D1500436

# GUY SAVOY

## SIMPLE FRENCH RECIPES
## FOR THE HOME COOK

FOREWORD BY PATRICIA WELLS

PHOTOGRAPHY BY LAURENCE MOUTON

STYLING BY CORINE MORIN

TRANSLATION BY ANNE DE RAVEL

Stewart, Tabori & Chang

New York

# FOREWORD

I first met Guy Savoy in the early 1980s when he was part of a band of up-and-coming young chefs. Back then, Guy worked in a tiny kitchen in a small restaurant that bore his name, on the Rue Duret in the sixteenth arrondissement. He had one, maybe two assistants, and quickly became known for a style of cooking that was light, aesthetically appealing, and fashioned from the ingredients he loved best. It wasn't long before he received his first Michelin star. But most of all, Guy was famed for his signature green color—his astute use of fresh herbs and dishes filled with an avalanche of vegetables. In 1987, Guy happily took over the large and spacious dining room near the Arc de Triomphe, on Rue Troyon in the seventeenth arrondissement. Here, he continued to grow and grow and grow, astonishing us with truly original and unusual modern fare, until he was finally awarded his third Michelin star in 2002.

Although you will see Guy walking through the dining room in his starched chef's whites, he is actually a man of the soil, born in 1953 in a small village in the Isère, where his mother tended the local café and where his father was a municipal gardener. Vegetables and greens, the freshest of the fresh, were the rule. He not only searches out the best suppliers for his fish and his sausages, his meat and his game, his cheese and his wines, but he makes friends with all of them. His generosity is unbounded, and totally real.

Here—in a book designed exclusively for the home cook—his love and flair shine through with typical brilliance. He offers us classics such as the perfect Gratin Dauphinois or Macaroni and Cheese, as well as new creations such as Celeraic Soup with Mushrooms and a Cold Zucchini Soup with Fresh Herbs. More important are the typical French *astuces* or tips that will help make an ordinary dish a spectacular one. The mouth-watering photos make us want to run into the kitchen and cook! Thank you, Guy, for sharing your passions.

**Patricia Wells**

October 2003

# A NOSTALGIC SKETCHBOOK

After my last book, *La Cuisine de mes Bistrots,* I felt the need to reintroduce the art of home cooking. And just like my previous book, this one teaches how to succeed at what is simple and how to prepare something that is already so well known we've lost track of its secrets.

The magic of being a chef these days comes from the ability to offer diners a multitude of culinary styles. But we are in danger of losing sight of what is simple, so home cooking has now become a new frontier, an approach we have to learn all over again. The questions I am often asked are about the simple dishes: how to make the perfect sole meunière or a haricots verts salad with a crème fraîche dressing. Simplicity is the goal. Three lines of explanation—and few cooking classes—are all you need to understand and master these recipes, but one must write those three lines. And the results remain unique, even if it seems like we have seen the recipe a hundred times before, because the details are what make the difference. The seasonings and accompaniment ideas that you'll find in this book bring individuality to the dishes, accentuating the strength of the classics. Going back to the basics and enhancing them—that's what cooking is all about.

The recipes in this book are tied to my childhood, whether they come directly from my home or family bar in Bourgoin-Jallieu, or were conceived in the same spirit of the cooking of my childhood. They are dishes I cook at home, just as often as I cook a more modern cuisine. Ten people on Sunday around a côte de boeuf with french fries and a béarnaise sauce whisked at the last minute give me just as much pleasure as a truffle and artichoke soup or oysters in an icy nage. This is my personal cuisine, a nostalgic sketchbook. In fact, what are the dishes I remember the most? The Sunday roasted chicken with mashed potatoes from my youth, followed by an apple tart, have left me with powerful memories, and they'll do the same for you and your guests.

When I was a child, I immersed myself in simple gourmand sensations, and I have built my life as a chef upon them. To reunite those sensations by putting them into a book feels like describing or returning to a landscape that had disappeared. Indeed, I have enjoyed all these childhood dishes for years with great pleasure, but the pleasure was largely oblivious. It was a landscape I had in front of my eyes for so many years but never took the time to actually contemplate. To do so, I had to leave my family home. And, as I did finally come to an understanding, I have been able to contemplate many landscapes! As time goes by, these landscapes fascinate me more and more. I absorb all those in front of me, during my travels, and even in Paris. I now can appreciate the value of what often seems too accessible or too simple because it is so close.

We are wrong to think that the daily routine is ordinary. Always conditioned to look for the exceptional, we let go of the small miracles within our reach. All ingredients can be interesting: for example, we pay so little attention to the humble carrot that we have stopped imagining new ways of using it. But there are still more noble qualities in a freshly picked, beautiful carrot, than in a lobster from Brittany kept frozen for a long time.

I hope that this book will allow you to discover the concept of a timeless cuisine that can be used to support all other existing styles—the timeless cuisine that starts in the home kitchen. It is important for each of us to make our own observations and come to our own conclusions, but I do want you to understand that cooking should be simple; there is no need to go to extremes. You are not competing for a world champion title, nor are you passing an exam. Don't feel guilty if you fail at making a sole meunière once or twice; that's part of culinary training. You first have to get a feel for the dishes before you can succeed.

At the outset, I would like to clarify a false idea; that of the difficulty of making stews. We have started to forgo braising because it is thought to be complicated. However, long cooking doesn't necessarily translate into long recipes. Assembling the ingredients takes only a few minutes, and then we are free to do whatever we please while the dish is slowly cooking. A beef and carrot stew is easier to prepare then a trout "au bleu." That is part of the magic of cooking—low heat works for you, filling the house with delicious scents and bringing with it a joie de vivre and a sense of comfort.

Cooking is the art of transforming an ingredient, with all its history, into happiness. A chicken from Bresse, carefully selected and given quality feeds, raised with a dedicated patience according to precious traditions, carries far more history than a chicken raised in a commercial coop. As you prepare these recipes, keep in mind the history of the ingredients you have selected and are about to magically transform.

I hope that the gourmand memories from my childhood will dissolve all anxiety and bring happiness to your kitchen.

**Guy Savoy**

# CONTENTS

**appetizers**

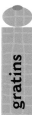
**gratins**

**fish**

Guy Savoy  Appetizers

# STEAMED GREEN ASPARAGUS
## WITH SAUCE LAURIS

2 pounds green asparagus

Salt

2 very fresh organic
egg yolks

Freshly ground black pepper

1 teaspoon Dijon mustard

1 cup grapeseed or
vegetable oil

2 tablespoons crème fraîche

1 tablespoon sweet paprika

2 tablespoons sherry
vinegar

1 tablespoon minced chives

Peel and trim the asparagus and gently rinse them under cold water.

Gather the asparagus into small bunches (about 6 asparagus per bunch) and tie them together with kitchen string. Holding the bunches firmly with one hand, bundle the string several times around the base of the spears, pulling the string up along the spears and tying them together just underneath the tips. Secure them with a loose double knot.

Bring 2 quarts of salted water to a boil in a large pot and gently add the asparagus. Place a kitchen towel over the water to retain the steam and ensure even cooking. Cook for about 5 minutes, or until just tender but still firm. To check for doneness, pierce the asparagus with a knife through the thickest part of the stem—you should encounter a slight resistance.

Carefully remove the asparagus from the water with tongs, making sure not to break them. Place them in ice water for a few seconds to stop them from cooking. Drain and dry the asparagus on a clean kitchen towel.

To make the sauce, place the egg yolks in a medium bowl. Add salt and pepper and whisk in the mustard. Slowly add the oil, a little at the time, whisking vigorously after each addition, until the mixture is fluffy and firm. Fold in the crème fraîche, paprika, and vinegar. Season with salt and pepper to taste.

You may serve the asparagus cold or plunge them in the hot cooking water for a few seconds to warm them before serving. Serve the sauce on the side garnished with chives.

*Lauris is a village in the Luberon region known for its asparagus. I learned how to make this sauce during my apprenticeship in the kitchens of Troisgros Restaurant in Roanne. The sauce should be thick, unctuous, and airy with a distinct vinegar flavor.*

# CELERAIC RÉMOULADE
## WITH SMOKED MAGRET

½ celeriac knob,
about 1½ pounds

1 cup crème fraîche

2 tablespoons old-fashioned
grainy mustard

2 tablespoons freshly
squeezed lemon juice

Salt and freshly ground
black pepper

16 slices smoked duck
magret (see Note)

8 thin slices aged
mimolette cheese (see Note)

4 chive sprigs

Balsamic vinegar
(optional)

Scrub and peel the celeriac. Cut it into a very fine julienne or shred it using a food processor or grater.

In a large bowl, combine the crème fraîche, mustard, and lemon juice. Season with salt and pepper to taste. Fold in the julienned celeriac, a little at a time, until well coated with the dressing. Refrigerate until ready to serve.

To serve, spoon some celeriac rémoulade in the center of 4 individual serving plates. Arrange 4 magret slices and 2 mimolette slices on top. Top with the chives. You may decorate the plates with a few dots of reduced balsamic vinegar, made by cooking the vinegar over low heat until it has been reduced by half.

*This flavorful recipe is a classic that has survived the test of time. The rémoulade is so simple to make, yet too often people choose the store-bought version rather than make their own. Here the magret and mimolette add luster and zest to the pale creaminess of the rémoulade.*

**Note:** Smoked duck magret is available in specialty stores and upscale supermarkets. It can also be ordered through d'Artagnan, Inc. (800-DARTAGN; www.dartagnan.com). If you can't find mimolette cheese, you can use slices of Parmesan instead.

# TUNA BROCHETTES
## WITH PIMENT D'ESPELETTE AND FENNEL

Rinse the tuna under cold running water. Dry with paper towels and cut into 1-inch cubes.

Combine 2 tablespoons of the olive oil and the Espelette pepper in a large dish. Add the tuna cubes and toss well to coat. Cover with plastic wrap and refrigerate for 30 minutes.

Wash the fennel bulbs and cut off the stems and any blemished outer leaves. Halve each bulb lengthwise and remove the hard center core. Cut crosswise into very thin slices.

Combine the fennel with ½ cup of the olive oil, vinegar, and thyme. Season with salt and pepper to taste, and marinate at room temperature until ready to serve.

Arrange the tuna on skewers. You should have 2 skewers with 5 pieces of tuna on each per person. Heat the remaining 6 tablespoons olive oil in a large frying pan. Add the skewers and cook for 1 to 2 minutes on each sides. Be careful not to overcook the tuna; it should remain pink at the center.

Spread the fennel salad on a serving platter. Place the skewers on top. You may garnish the dish with a sprinkling of minced chive or chervil.

One 1¼-pound tuna loin

1 cup extra-virgin olive oil

½ teaspoon ground Espelette pepper (see Note)

3 small fennel bulbs, about 1¼ pounds

¼ cup balsamic vinegar

½ teaspoon fresh thyme

Salt and freshly ground black pepper to taste

Minced chive or chervil (optional)

*The Espelette pepper spices up the flavor of the tuna and works with its dense texture; it also adds some heat while the fennel is cooling. Fennel is not often used in cooking and yet it is so flavorful and easy to work with. Keep it in mind for an accompaniment that is simple and unusual.*

**Note:** Piment d'Espelette is a pepper grown in the Basque region of France. It is mildly hot with subtle sweet undertones, and it can be found in gourmet stores.

# GREEN BEAN SALAD
## WITH CREAM

1¼ pound tender green
beans or haricots verts

Salt

1 shallot

Juice of 1 lemon

Freshly ground black
pepper

½ cup crème fraîche

1 small bunch chives

Snap off the tops and ends of the beans and remove the strings. Rinse the beans in a colander under cold running water.

Bring a large pot of salted water to a boil, add the beans, and cook for 6 to 8 minutes, or until tender but still slightly crisp. Drain and rinse under cold running water. Refrigerate until ready to serve.

Mince the shallot. In a medium bowl, combine the lemon juice and salt and pepper to taste. Stir well to dissolve the salt. Stir in the minced shallot and crème fraîche. Refrigerate dressing until ready to serve.

Just before serving, combine the beans with the dressing. Arrange on individual serving plates, and garnish with chive sprigs.

 *This crème fraîche and lemon dressing is versatile and faster to prepare than vinaigrette, and it can be used in many salads such as potato salad. The green beans should not be marinated; the dressing should be added just before serving. This salad is best served slightly chilled.*

# DANDELION SALAD
## WITH POACHED EGG

1 pound dandelion greens

¼ cup balsamic vinegar

Salt and freshly ground black pepper

½ cup walnut oil

½ cup grapeseed or vegetable oil

1 tablespoon white vinegar

4 very fresh organic eggs

4 ounces fresh walnuts in the shell

4 ounces fresh hazelnuts in the shell

2 sprigs Italian parsley, minced

Trim and wash the dandelions; dry well.

In a medium bowl, combine the balsamic vinegar and salt and pepper to taste. Stir well to dissolve the salt. Whisk in the walnut and grapeseed oils until the mixture has emulsified.

In a large pot, bring 1 quart of water to a boil. Add the white vinegar. Lower the heat and bring down to a low simmer. Break each egg into a small cup or ramekin and then carefully slide them into the simmering water. The whites should not separate from the yolks. Using a spoon, gently fold the whites over the yolks, making sure they don't break. Check for doneness after 1 minute by poking the eggs with the tip of your finger. The yolks should remain soft with the whites cooked through and firm. Gently remove the eggs with a slotted spoon and place them in a large bowl of cold water.

In a large bowl, toss the dandelions with the vinaigrette. Shell and peel the nuts, and chop them coarsely.

Divide the dandelion salad among 4 individual serving plates or spread on a large platter. Carefully nestle the poached eggs on top of the greens. Just before serving, sprinkle with the chopped nuts and the parsley.

*Fresh walnuts and hazelnuts remind me of my childhood home and the groves surrounding it. When this salad was served, I was careful to dig deep into the bottom of the salad bowl where most of the poached egg pieces were hiding.*

# CHANTERELLE FRICASSEE
## WITH SEASONAL GREENS

12 ounces chanterelle mushrooms

1 small head Boston lettuce

1 small head frisée lettuce or an equal amount of the tender part of curly endive

2 cups loosely packed red or green oak leaf lettuce

1 small head radicchio

8 tablespoons unsalted butter

Salt

1 shallot, minced

2 sprigs Italian parsley, minced

Freshly ground black pepper

½ cup Basic Vinaigrette (see recipe, page 50)

Cut off the stems of the chanterelles and scrape off any blemishes with a paring knife. Rinse the chanterelles quickly under cold water, taking care not to break them. Drain well and dry on paper towels.

Trim and wash the lettuces; dry well.

Melt 2 tablespoons of the butter in a large skillet over medium heat. Sprinkle with salt and raise the heat to high. Add the chanterelles and sauté, stirring occasionally, for about 3 minutes, or until softened. Remove from the pan and drain in a colander set over a small saucepan, reserving the mushrooms.

Reduce the chanterelle juices by half over medium heat. Whisk in 4 tablespoons of the butter, a few pieces at a time, until the sauce is smooth and silky. Keep warm.

Heat the remaining 2 tablespoons butter in a small skillet over high heat. Add the chanterelles and sauté until golden. Add the shallot and cook for 30 seconds longer. Toss with the parsley and remove from the heat. Season with salt and pepper to taste.

Toss to combine the lettuces with the vinaigrette in a large mixing bowl.

Just before serving, emulsify the cooking liquid using an immersion blender or in the bowl of a blender. Divide the salad among 4 individual serving plates. Scatter the chanterelles over each plate and spoon the sauce around the edges. Serve immediately.

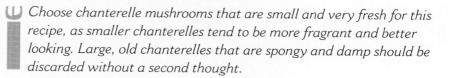

*Choose chanterelle mushrooms that are small and very fresh for this recipe, as smaller chanterelles tend to be more fragrant and better looking. Large, old chanterelles that are spongy and damp should be discarded without a second thought.*

# ARUGULA
## AND SQUID SALAD

Clean the squid under cold running water. Cut the squid into ¼-inch slices and drain on paper towels. Refrigerate until ready to use.

Trim and wash the arugula. Coarsely chop the pistachios and set aside about ½ tablespoon for garnish.

In a medium bowl, combine the pistachios, vinegar, and salt and pepper to taste. Add ½ cup of the olive oil in a slow stream, whisking constantly until emulsified. Set aside.

Heat the remaining ¼ cup olive oil in a large skillet over very high heat. Add the squid and cook briefly until it becomes stiff and lightly golden, about 5 minutes. Drain in a colander.

Set aside 2 tablespoons of the vinaigrette and toss the rest with the arugula in a medium bowl. Divide the salad among 4 individual serving plates, top with the squid, and drizzle the remaining dressing on top. Garnish with the reserved pistachios.

½ pound squid

¼ pound baby arugula

2 tablespoons pistachio nuts

1 tablespoon balsamic vinegar

Salt and freshly ground black pepper

¾ cup extra-virgin olive oil

*Make sure to cook the squid very quickly or it will become tough. In this recipe the squid is both tender and crunchy, and it is lightly coated with the dressing. The peppery flavors of the arugula spice up the dish.*

# SAUSAGE
## EN BRIOCHE

Serves 6 to 8

Preparation Time: **1 hour the day before + 2 hours the day of serving**

Cooking Time: **35 minutes the day before + 20 minutes the day of serving**

**For the sausage:**

1 medium carrot

1 medium onion

1 celery stalk

1 cup white wine

¼ bay leaf

1 sprig thyme

10 black peppercorns

1 garlic sausage, about 8 inches long and 2½ inches thick (see Sources, page 191)

**For the brioche:**

1 package active dry yeast, 1½ teaspoons

1 teaspoon sugar

1½ cups all-purpose flour

Pinch salt

2 whole eggs, beaten

1 egg yolk, beaten

4 tablespoons unsalted butter, at room temperature

**For the sauce:**

1 shallot

¼ cup port wine

1 cup veal stock (see recipe, page 137)

2 tablespoons unsalted butter

**The Day Before:** To make the stock, cut the carrot, onion, and celery into chunks. Bring 6 cups of water to a boil in a large pot. Add the white wine, carrot, onion, celery, bay leaf, thyme, and peppercorns. Reduce the heat and simmer for 15 minutes.

Wrap the sausage in plastic wrap. Poke a few holes through the plastic wrap without piercing the sausage. Place the sausage into the pot with the stock and simmer for 20 minutes. Remove the sausage, let it cool, and refrigerate overnight.

**The Day of Serving:** To make the brioche dough, place the yeast, sugar, and 2 tablespoons of the flour in a small mixing bowl and whisk in ¼ cup tepid water. Set aside in a warm place for 5 to 10 minutes, until the mixture bubbles and foams.

Combine the remaining flour with the salt in a large mixing bowl and make a well in the center. Add 1 of the beaten eggs, the egg yolk, and yeast mixture and mix with a wooden spoon. Add the butter and knead until the dough is soft, shiny, and elastic, about 10 minutes. If you prefer, the dough can be prepared in a food processor or an electric mixer fitted with a dough hook. Cover the bowl with a damp kitchen towel and set aside in a warm place for about 2 hours, or until the dough has doubled in bulk. Push down on the dough to deflate it and knead briefly.

Preheat the oven to 400°F. Lightly butter a 4-cup loaf pan. Take the sausage out of the refrigerator, unwrap it, and remove the casing. Roll out the dough into a 10-inch square. Wrap the dough around the sausage and place it seam side down into the loaf pan.

In a small bowl, beat the remaining egg with 1 tablespoon of water. Brush the mixture over the dough. Place in the oven and bake for 20 minutes, until golden.

Meanwhile, prepare the sauce. Mince the shallot and place it with the port in a small saucepan over medium heat. Cook until the liquid is almost evaporated. Add the veal stock, bring it to a boil, and remove the pan from the heat. Whisk in the butter, a few pieces at the time, until well blended and smooth. Strain the sauce into a sauceboat. Cut the sausage en brioche into 1-inch slices and serve with the port sauce.

*In my family sausage en brioche was served as a first course on special occasions. It was our foie gras! This recipe is somewhat more complicated than most of the other recipes in the book, but well worth the effort. The weight of the sausage should be equal to that of the dough.*

# POT-AU-FEU SALAD

Serves 4

Preparation Time: 2½ hours
the day before + 1½ hours
the day of serving

Cooking Time: 3½ hours
the day before serving

**The Day Before:** Trim and wash the leek and cut the leek, carrots, and celery into large chunks. Halve the onions. Fill a large stockpot with 3 quarts of water, add the short ribs, and bring to a boil. Using a slotted spoon, skim off any foam that forms at the top. Add the vegetables, bouquet garni, and coarse salt. Return to a boil, lower the heat, and simmer for 1½ hours. Add the beef shank and cook for 2 more hours.

Remove the meat and onions from the broth and set aside to cool. Strain the broth through a chinois or a fine-mesh strainer and set aside to cool. Discard the other vegetables. Refrigerate the meat, onions, and broth separately overnight.

**The Day of Serving:** Remove the meat, onions, and broth from the refrigerator and allow them to come to room temperature. Wash the spinach and discard any tough stems.

Shred the meat. Discard the bones and any fatty parts. Coarsely mince the reserved onions and combine them with the ribs and shank. Moisten the mixture with some broth to give it a soft, smooth consistency. Mince the shallots. Finely dice the cornichons. In a large bowl, combine the shallots and cornichons with the shredded meat and refrigerate for 1 hour.

In a medium bowl, toss the spinach with the vinaigrette, and place in the center of 4 individual serving plates. Adjust the seasonings of the pot-au-feu with salt and pepper. Using 2 large spoons, shape the mixture into quenelles (see photo, opposite) and arrange them around the spinach salad.

For the pot-au-feu:

1 leek

2 medium carrots

1 celery stalk

3 medium onions

1 pound beef short ribs

Bouquet garni (¼ bay leaf, 2 sprigs Italian parsley, 1 sprig thyme), tied in cheesecloth

1 tablespoon coarse salt

1 pound beef shank

Salt and freshly ground black pepper

For the salad:

¾ pound baby spinach

2 shallots

8 cornichons

⅓ cup Basic Vinaigrette (see recipe, page 50)

*This dish also works well with leftover pot-au-feu—you only need to make the spinach salad. I've used cooked onions here instead of the traditional raw ones, which don't agree with everyone.*

# VEGETABLE AND BACON
## QUICHE

**For the crust:**

2 cups all-purpose flour

Pinch salt

1 egg yolk, beaten

8 tablespoons unsalted butter, chilled and diced

2 tablespoons water, if necessary

**For the filling:**

2 medium zucchini

⅓ cup olive oil

4 small fennel bulbs

4 medium tomatoes

4 ounces slab bacon

2 whole eggs

2 egg yolks

¼ cup milk

¾ cup heavy cream

Salt and freshly ground black pepper

Sift the flour and salt into a large mixing bowl and create a well in the center. Add the beaten egg yolk to the well and stir it into the flour with a fork. Using your fingers, quickly rub the butter into the flour until the mixture is still crumbly and just holds together. If it looks too dry, add some water, 1 teaspoon at a time. Gather the dough into a ball and place it on a lightly floured work surface. Knead for 2 to 3 minutes, or until smooth. Wrap the dough in plastic and refrigerate for 1 hour.

Meanwhile, cut the zucchini into ¼-inch cubes. Heat half of the olive oil in a skillet and sauté the zucchini until golden, about 5 minutes. Drain and set aside. Remove the stems and hard center core of the fennel bulbs. Cut crosswise into thin slices.

Combine the remaining olive oil with 1 cup of water in a medium saucepan. Add the fennel, cover, and cook over medium-low heat for 30 minutes, or until tender. Pass the fennel through a food mill or puree it in a food processor. Return the puree to the saucepan and cook, stirring occasionally, over low heat until the liquid has evaporated.

Bring a small pot of water to a boil. Score the skin of the tomatoes and plunge them into the water for a few seconds. Remove the tomatoes to a colander and rinse. Peel and seed the tomatoes and cut them into ½-inch cubes. Cut the bacon into ½-inch by 1-inch pieces. Blanch for a few seconds in the hot water and drain into a colander.

Preheat the oven to 350°F.

Combine the eggs, egg yolks, milk, cream, and salt and pepper to taste in a large mixing bowl and set aside.

Roll the dough into a ⅛-inch thick circle. Line a 12-inch tart mold with the dough, pressing gently along the sides and bottom to set it in place. Trim the excess dough to around ½ inch all around. Cover the bottom of the mold with aluminum foil. Fill with dried beans or a baking pallet. Bake for 12 minutes. Remove the beans and foil and bake for another 5 minutes. Fill the pastry shell with the fennel puree, vegetables, and bacon. Pour in the egg mixture and bake for 20 to 30 minutes, until the filling is set and the top is golden brown.

*In my family, savory tarts or quiches, so easy to make and so fragrant when they come out of the oven, were served on special occasions. This variation with its Mediterranean-style filling is a pleasant change from the usual quiche Lorraine or leek tart.*

# MONKFISH TERRINE

4 large onions, sliced

Salt

2 small Savoy cabbages

5 medium carrots

5 medium zucchini

⅓ cup olive oil

1 pound monkfish fillets

Freshly ground black pepper

Place 2 onions in a large saucepan, sprinkle with salt, and add just enough cold water to cover. Braise for 2 hours over low heat until the onions form a smooth, creamy puree. Set aside to cool. Bring a large pot of salted water to a boil. Fill a mixing bowl with cold water and add a few ice cubes. Trim and quarter the cabbage, dicarding the core. Cut the carrots and zucchini into 4-inch by ½-inch sticks. Blanch the cabbage in the boiling water for 5 minutes. Remove with a slotted spoon and plunge into the ice bath and then drain. Add the carrot to the boiling water and cook for 2 to 3 minutes, or until just tender. Remove them to the ice bath, then drain. Add the zucchini to the boiling water and cook about 2 minutes, until just tender. Remove them to the ice bath and drain.

Heat the oil in a large skillet, add the monkfish, and sauté over medium heat until just cooked through and golden on all sides, 4 to 5 minutes. Season with salt and pepper to taste.

Coarsely chop the cabbage. Arrange a layer of carrots and zucchini at the bottom of a 9-inch terrine mold. Spread some of the cabbage on top and then add some of the onion puree. Repeat until the mold is half full. Place the monkfish on top of the vegetables and continue filling the mold in alternating layers. Cover the mold with plastic wrap and place a heavy weight on top. Refrigerate for at least 6 hours. To serve, unmold the terrine onto a serving platter and cut into 1-inch slices.

*This terrine makes an attractive first course. It is chic, distinctive, and flavorful yet still very simple. I suggest serving it with a well-seasoned fresh herb salad sprinkled with fleur de sel or coarse sea salt.*

# SARDINES
## ESCABECHE

16 very fresh sardines

3 lemons

1 quart vegetable stock

¼ cup white wine vinegar

Salt and freshly ground
black pepper

1 small bunch chives,
minced

Ask your fishmonger to clean and fillet the sardines.

Using a sharp knife, peel the lemons, cutting deep to expose the pulp. Cut the peeled lemons into very thin slices.

Combine the vegetable stock and vinegar in a flameproof baking dish large enough to hold the sardines in a single layer. Bring the mixture just to a boil and remove from the heat.

Arrange the sardines in the dish. Season with salt and pepper to taste and cover with the lemon slices. Return the mixture to a boil. Remove from the heat and allow to cool. Cover with plastic and refrigerate for 2 hours.

Remove the escabeche from the refrigerator and sprinkle with the chives. Serve very cold.

*This light appetizer can be served with* cervelle de canut *(a specialty from Lyon made from a fresh white cheese fresh herbs, and minced shallots). Fresh anchovies or bluefish may be substituted for the sardines. The lemon slices in this dish lend their subtle aroma to the fish.*

# WHITE BEAN SALAD
## WITH FRESH HERBS

Soak the beans in cold water overnight. Drain the beans and place them in a stockpot with the chicken stock, carrot, onion, and bouquet garni. Cover with 2 quarts of water. Bring to a boil, lower the heat, and simmer for 45 minutes, or until the bean have softened. Season with salt during the last 10 minutes of cooking.

Reserve about ¼ cup of the cooking liquid and drain the beans. Discard the bouquet garni. Place the beans in a large bowl and stir in the vinegar, oil, and reserved cooking liquid. Add salt and pepper to taste. Mince the parsley and chervil, and cut the chives into ¼-inch sticks. Sprinkle the herbs over the beans and serve.

*This salad is best served at room temperature or slightly warm, along with some hazelnut bread. I like coco beans for their softness and delicate flavor, but you may use any type of beans, keeping in mind that more dressing may be needed depending on the starchiness of the beans.*

**Note:** French coco beans are available in gourmet and specialty food stores.

½ pound dried coco beans (see Note)

½ cup chicken stock (see recipe, page 136)

1 medium carrot, diced

1 medium onion, diced

Bouquet garni (1 sprig thyme, 1 bay leaf, 1 small leek, green parts only), tied in cheesecloth

Salt

¼ cup sherry vinegar

½ cup hazelnut oil

Fresh herbs: Italian parsley, chervil, chives

Freshly ground black pepper

# SCALLOPS
## IN A LEMONGRASS NAGE

Peel the carrot and onions. Trim the lemongrass. Pound lightly with the back of a chef's knife to crush and cut in half lengthwise.

Combine the vinegar, 2½ cups water, bouquet garni, carrot, onion, and lemongrass in a large saucepan. Season with the coarse salt and peppercorns. Bring to a boil, lower the heat, and simmer for 30 minutes.

Rinse the scallops in a colander under cold running water. Dry on paper towels. Discard the stems from the lemon balm and mince the leaves. Set aside. Poach the scallops in the broth for 2 minutes; do not overcook. Remove with a slotted spoon and keep warm.

Strain the broth and return it to the saucepan. Discard the bouquet garni and lemongrass. Reserve the carrot and onion slices. Heat the broth over low heat and whisk in the butter, a few pieces at a time. The mixture should be smooth and emulsified. Season with salt and pepper to taste. Arrange the scallops and reserved carrots and onions in 4 individual soup bowls. Ladle the broth over them. Garnish with a sprinkling of lemon balm.

1 medium carrot

5 ounces pearl onions

5 stalks lemongrass

½ cup white wine vinegar

Bouquet garni (¼ bay leaf, 2 sprigs Italian parsley, 1 sprig thyme), wrapped in cheesecloth

1 teaspoon coarse salt

½ teaspoon white peppercorns

20 large scallops

1 bunch lemon balm

4 tablespoons unsalted butter

Salt and freshly ground white pepper

*This is a fragrant light appetizer, which sets itself apart with the distinct flavors and delicate freshness of the lemon balm and lemongrass.*

# MUSSEL
## SOUP

2¼ pounds small mussels

2 shallots

1 cup white wine

1½ cups fish stock (see recipe, page 96)

¾ cup crème fraîche

Salt and freshly ground black pepper

Optional Garnishes:

Chervil leaves

Diced zucchini marinated in olive oil for 1 hour

Use a paring knife to scrape off the mussel shells and pull off the beards. Wash the mussels several times in cold water and drain. Keep refrigerated until ready to use. Coarsely chop the shallots.

Warm a large pot over high heat for about 2 minutes, or until the pot is very hot. Add the mussels, wine, and shallots. Cover and cook for a few minutes, stirring occasionally, until the mussels open. Remove the mussels from the pot and set aside. Reserve the cooking liquid.

In another large pot, bring the fish stock to a boil. Strain the reserved cooking juices from the mussels into the stock. Add the crème fraîche and bring it just to a boil. Remove from the heat. Add salt if necessary (taste the mussels first; they usually are very salty) and pepper to taste. Set aside.

Remove the mussels from their shells and divide them among 4 individual soup bowls. Ladle the warm soup over them.

You may garnish the soup with the chervil leaves or marinated zucchini.

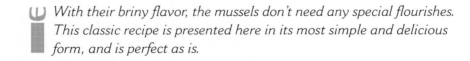

*With their briny flavor, the mussels don't need any special flourishes. This classic recipe is presented here in its most simple and delicious form, and is perfect as is.*

# COLD ZUCCHINI SOUP
## WITH FRESH HERBS

Trim the zucchini and cut them into thin slices.

Heat the olive oil in a large pot over medium heat. Add the zucchini and cook over medium-low heat, stirring constantly, for about 2 minutes, or until the zucchini are soft but not brown. Add 1 quart water and the coarse salt, and bring to a boil. Lower the heat and simmer until the zucchini are very soft, about 15 minutes. Puree the mixture in a food processor until smooth, pour the soup into a large bowl, and set aside to cool. Season with salt and pepper to taste and refrigerate for 2 hours. Just before serving, mince the chervil, parsley, and mint and sprinkle them over the soup.

10 small zucchini, about 2 ounces each

2 tablespoons olive oil

1 teaspoon coarse salt

Salt and freshly ground black pepper

10 chervil leaves

10 Italian parsley leaves

4 mint leaves

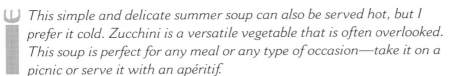

*This simple and delicate summer soup can also be served hot, but I prefer it cold. Zucchini is a versatile vegetable that is often overlooked. This soup is perfect for any meal or any type of occasion—take it on a picnic or serve it with an apéritif.*

# CREAM OF PUMPKIN SOUP
## WITH SWEET GARLIC

1 head garlic

3 cups milk

1 small pumpkin, about
1½ pounds

2 tablespoons unsalted
butter

1 cup chicken stock
(see recipe, page 136)

1 cup heavy cream

Salt and freshly ground
black pepper to taste

1 small bunch parsley,
minced

Peel the garlic cloves and set aside 2 to make the garlic chips. Place the remaining cloves in a small saucepan along with 1½ cups of the milk. Bring just to a boil, then remove from the heat and drain, discarding the milk. Repeat with the remaining 1½ cups milk.

Peel the pumpkin and discard the fiber and seeds. Cut the flesh into 1-inch cubes.

Warm the butter in a large pot and add the pumpkin cubes and blanched garlic cloves. Cook over high heat, stirring often and crushing the flesh of the pumpkin as it becomes soft. Add the chicken stock, lower the heat to medium-low, and simmer for about 40 minutes, or until the pumpkin is very tender. Add the cream and cook for 6 to 7 minutes. Puree the mixture in a food processor until smooth and pour the soup into a large bowl. Season with salt and pepper to taste.

Preheat oven to 250°F. To make the garlic chips, thinly slice the remaining cloves and place them on a baking sheet. Place them in the oven and bake for 5 minutes, until golden and crisp. Ladle the soup into heated soup bowls. Sprinkle with garlic chips and parsley.

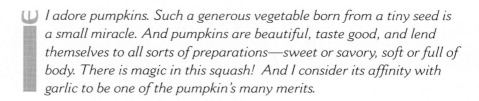

*I adore pumpkins. Such a generous vegetable born from a tiny seed is a small miracle. And pumpkins are beautiful, taste good, and lend themselves to all sorts of preparations—sweet or savory, soft or full of body. There is magic in this squash! And I consider its affinity with garlic to be one of the pumpkin's many merits.*

# CELERAIC SOUP
## WITH MUSHROOMS

¾ pound celeriac

1 medium leek

Bouquet garni (¼ bay leaf, 2 sprigs Italian parsley, 1 sprig thyme), tied in cheesecloth

2½ quarts chicken stock (see recipe, page 136)

½ pound white mushrooms

1 tablespoon unsalted butter

Salt and freshly ground black pepper

Parsley or chervil leaves for garnish

Scrub and peel the celeriac and cut it into 1-inch cubes. Cut off most of the green part of the leek removing the root and any blemished leaves. Insert a sharp paring knife about 2 inches above the root and cut through the entire length of the leek. Wash thoroughly under running water. Cut crosswise into slices. Place the celeriac and leek in a large pot along with the bouquet garni. Add the chicken stock and bring to a boil. Lower the heat and simmer for 20 minutes, until the celeriac is very tender. Wash then thinly slice the mushrooms. Heat the butter in a skillet over medium heat, add the mushrooms, and cook until golden, about 5 minutes. Drain and set aside. Remove the bouquet garni from the soup. Puree the soup in a food processor until smooth and pour into a large bowl. Season with salt and pepper. Just before serving, add the mushrooms and garnish with parsley or chervil.

*For a more elegant first course, substitute cèpes, oyster mushrooms, chanterelles, or shiitakes for the white mushrooms.*

# COLD CARROT SOUP
## WITH STAR ANISE
## AND MOZZARELLA

Cut the mozzarella into sticks, place them in a small bowl with the olive oil, and leave them to marinate until ready to use. Cut the carrots into ½-inch slices.

Heat 3 tablespoons of the butter in a large pot. Add the carrot slices and cook, covered, over low heat for 3 to 4 minutes, or until the carrots start to wilt. Do not allow them to brown. Add the chicken stock and cream. Bring to a boil, lower the heat, and simmer, covered, for 1 hour. Turn off the heat, add the star anise, cover, and let sit for 20 to 30 minutes. Remove the star anise and puree the soup in a food processor until smooth. Stir in the remaining 1 tablespoon butter and add salt and pepper to taste. Pour the soup into a large bowl and refrigerate for 2 hours. Arrange the marinated mozzarella sticks on top of the soup just before serving.

*An herb or spice associated with a familiar type of produce can bring out some unsuspected qualities. For example, here the star anise is in harmony with the humble carrot. You may also experiment with other herbs such as mint or tarragon.*

¼ pound fresh mozzarella

1 cup olive oil

1 pound carrots

4 tablespoons unsalted butter

2½ cups chicken stock

2½ cups heavy cream

4 star anise

Salt and freshly ground black pepper

# OXTAIL
## TERRINE

1 medium carrot

1 medium onion

1 celery stalk

1¼ pounds oxtail

Bouquet garni (¼ bay leaf, 2 sprigs Italian parsley, 1 sprig thyme), tied in cheesecloth

Salt

1 shallot, minced

2 teaspoons sherry vinegar

Freshly ground black pepper

Juice of 1 lemon

2 artichokes, trimmed

4 teaspoons grapeseed or vegetable oil

Cut the carrot, onion, and celery into large chunks. Place them in a large pot along with the oxtail and bouquet garni. Cover with 2 quarts of water, season with salt, and bring to a boil. Lower heat and simmer for 3 hours. The meat should be tender and pull easily from the bones. Remove the oxtail, and carrot, and onion and set aside to cool. Discard the broth with the celery.

When the oxtail is cool enough to handle, remove the meat from the bones and shred it, discarding the bones and fatty pieces. In a large bowl, combine the meat with the shallot and 1 teaspoon of the vinegar. Season with salt and pepper to taste.

Layer half of the oxtail mixture into a 4-cup terrine mold. Layer some of the reserved carrot and onion pieces on top and cover with the remaining mixture. Press down lightly. Cover the mold with plastic wrap and refrigerate for at least 12 hours.

Bring 2 quarts of salted water to a boil. Add the lemon juice and the artichokes and cook for 40 minutes, or until tender. Remove the artichokes from the pot and set aside to cool. Carefully peel off the leaves and remove the choke with a spoon. Place the artichoke bottoms in a mortar or mixing bowl. Add the remaining teaspoon of vinegar and pound the artichokes to a fine puree. Whisk in the oil, a little at a time, until the mixture is creamy. Season with salt and pepper. Remove the terrine from the refrigerator, cut it into ¾-inch slices and place on individual serving plates. Drizzle with the artichoke vinaigrette.

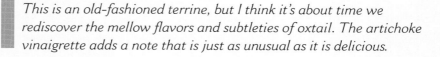

*This is an old-fashioned terrine, but I think it's about time we rediscover the mellow flavors and subtleties of oxtail. The artichoke vinaigrette adds a note that is just as unusual as it is delicious.*

# WARM CHICKEN LIVER MOUSSE WITH QUENELLES AND
## TOMATO-MUSHROOM SAUCE

For the sauce:

8 large tomatoes

2 shallots, minced

1 garlic clove, minced

Bouquet garni (¼ bay leaf, 2 sprigs Italian parsley, 1 sprig thyme), tied in cheesecloth

Salt and freshly ground black pepper

½ pound white mushrooms

1 tablespoon extra-virgin olive oil

For the quenelles:

8 tablespoons unsalted butter

Salt

3⅔ cups flour, plus extra to roll out the dough

4 eggs

**Make the sauce:** Bring a large pot of water to a boil. Score the skin of the tomatoes with a sharp knife, and plunge the tomatoes in the water for a few seconds. Remove the tomatoes to a colander and rinse them under cold running water. Peel and seed the tomatoes and finely dice the flesh.

Place the shallots in a large saucepan over medium heat and cook for few seconds. Add the tomatoes, garlic, and bouquet garni. Season with salt and pepper, cover, reduce the heat to low, and cook for 30 minutes. Remove the bouquet garni and adjust the seasonings to taste.

Thinly slice the mushrooms. Heat the oil in a medium skillet over high heat, add the mushrooms, and sauté until lightly golden. Drain in a colander set over a bowl. Add the mushroom juices to the tomato sauce.

**Make the quenelles:** Combine 2½ cups water and the 8 tablespoons butter in a large pot. Add a pinch of salt and bring to a boil. Remove from the heat and add the flour at once, beating the mixture vigorously with a wooden spoon until well blended. Return the pot to low heat for a few minutes, stirring constantly, to "dry" the dough. The dough should be soft smooth, and not sticky. When the dough starts pulling away from the sides of the pot, remove the pot from the heat, pour the dough into a large mixing bowl, and let it cool for few minutes. Add the eggs, one at a time, beating and blending in between each addition. The mixture should be thick and shiny. Set aside until ready to use.

**Make the mousse:** Preheat the oven to 300°F. Puree the liver in a food processor. Add the whole egg, yolk, and cream. Season with salt and pepper. Blend until well combined. Strain through a chinois or fine-mesh strainer. Set aside.

Brush the bottom and sides of four 1-cup ramekins with the ½ tablespoon melted butter. Divide the chicken mixture equally among the ramekins. Place the ramekins in a baking dish and pour in enough boiling water to come halfway up the sides. Bake for 20 to 25 minutes, or until the custard is firm. Remove the baking dish from the oven and cover with a sheet of aluminum foil. Set aside.

Increase the oven temperature to 350°F. Bring a large pot of salted water to a boil.

Lightly flour a work surface. Divide the quenelle dough into small balls about the size of golf balls and roll them with the palm of your hand to form sticks about 3⅓-inch long and ¾-inch wide. Coat the sticks with flour as you go along. Place the sticks in the water and cook for 30 seconds, or until they rise to the surface. Remove with a slotted spoon and drain on paper towels.

Pour the tomato sauce into a baking dish large enough to hold the quenelles in a single layer. Add the mushrooms. Arrange the quenelles over the mushrooms and bake for 15 minutes.

Unmold the ramekins, place the mousse on individual serving plates, spoon some of the tomato sauce on top, and arrange the quenelles around the mousse.

*This is another childhood recipe that my mother prepared, a perfect example of regional home cooking. Our quenelles were in fact long gnocchi, made with cream-puff dough and shaped by hand. They were prepared with a tomato and mushroom sauce and served with the warm chicken liver mousse.*

For the mousse:

¾ pound chicken liver, trimmed

1 whole egg

1 egg yolk

2 cups heavy cream

Salt and freshly ground black pepper

½ tablespoon melted butter

2 tablespoons unsalted butter

# CREAMY LENTILS WITH
## SAUTÉED DUCK FOIE GRAS

½ pound green lentils

1 medium onion

1 whole clove

1 medium carrot

1 sprig Italian parsley, minced

1 sprig thyme, minced

¼ bay leaf

Coarse salt

Freshly ground black pepper to taste

Salt

½ cup heavy cream

½ pound fresh duck foie gras

1 tablespoon balsamic vinegar

Italian parsley leaves for garnish

Place the lentils in a large pot and cover with cold water. Bring to a boil, then remove from the heat and drain. Stud the onion with the clove. Return the lentils to the pot along with the carrot, onion, parsley, thyme, and bay leaf. Cover with cold water, season with coarse salt and pepper, and bring to a boil. Reduce the heat, cover, and simmer for 25 minutes, or until the lentils are tender.

Drain the lentils in a colander set over a bowl and discard the vegetables and herbs. Reserve the cooking liquid. Puree the lentils, adding some of the cooking liquid if the mixture looks too dry. Press the puree through a fine-mesh strainer. The puree should be smooth.

Place the lentil puree in a medium saucepan, add a little cooking liquid to smooth it out, stir in the cream, and bring it to a boil. Reduce the heat to low and simmer for a few minutes. Season with salt and pepper to taste. Keep warm.

Cut the foie gras into ½-inch-thick slices. Lightly season with salt and pepper on both sides. Heat a heavy skillet over medium-high heat. Sauté the foie gras slices for 30 seconds on each side. Remove from the pan and keep warm. Deglaze the pan with the balsamic and drizzle the liquid over the foie gras.

Divide the lentils among 4 individual serving plates, top with a slice of foie gras, and garnish with the parsley.

*Lentils are my favorite legume. They have a magnificent flavor and make a subtle accompaniment to a variety of ingredients. To me, lentils are as precious as foie gras, which makes their association in this recipe a success. Forget the school-cafeteria lentils and their stones from when we were young; it's time to welcome this noble and inviting ingredient, so accommodating and easy to cook.*

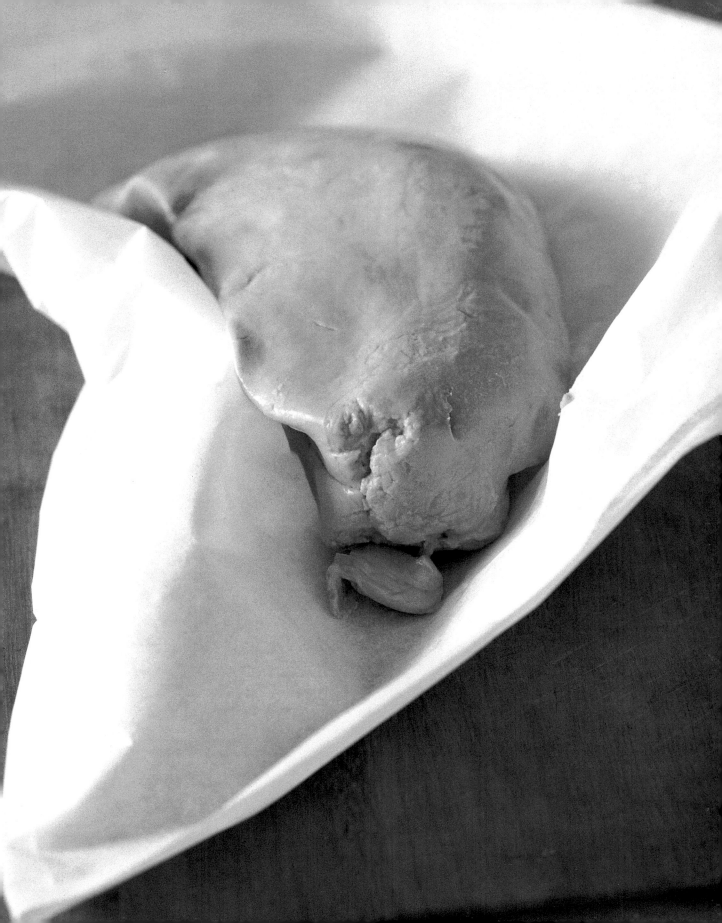

# BASIC VINAIGRETTE

1 tablespoon sherry vinegar

Salt and freshly ground black pepper

1 teaspoon Dijon mustard

½ cup grapeseed or vegetable oil

Combine the vinegar and salt and pepper to taste in a medium bowl. Whisk until the salt is dissolved.

Whisk in the mustard. Slowly add the oil in a steady stream, whisking constantly, until the ingredients emulsify. The vinaigrette should be well blended and smooth. Refrigerate until ready to use.

To further emulsify the vinaigrette, blend the vinaigrette in a blender along with 1 tablespoon of water.

*This vinaigrette can also be made with olive oil, or you can use hazelnut, walnut, or another type of flavored oil. When using flavored oils, use about one part flavored oil to ten parts grapeseed oil. Choose the oil according to the other ingredients and preparation you're using. Hazelnut vinaigrette, for example, goes well with poultry and squab, and olive oil goes well with fish.*

# HERB-FLAVORED OIL

Place the chives, chervil, and parsley in the bowl of a food processor or blender. Add salt and pepper to taste. With the machine running, add the oil in a slow, steady stream. Store in a jar with a tight-fitting lid and refrigerate until ready to use.

½ bunch chives

¼ bunch chervil

¼ bunch Italian parsley

Salt and freshly ground black pepper

½ cup olive oil

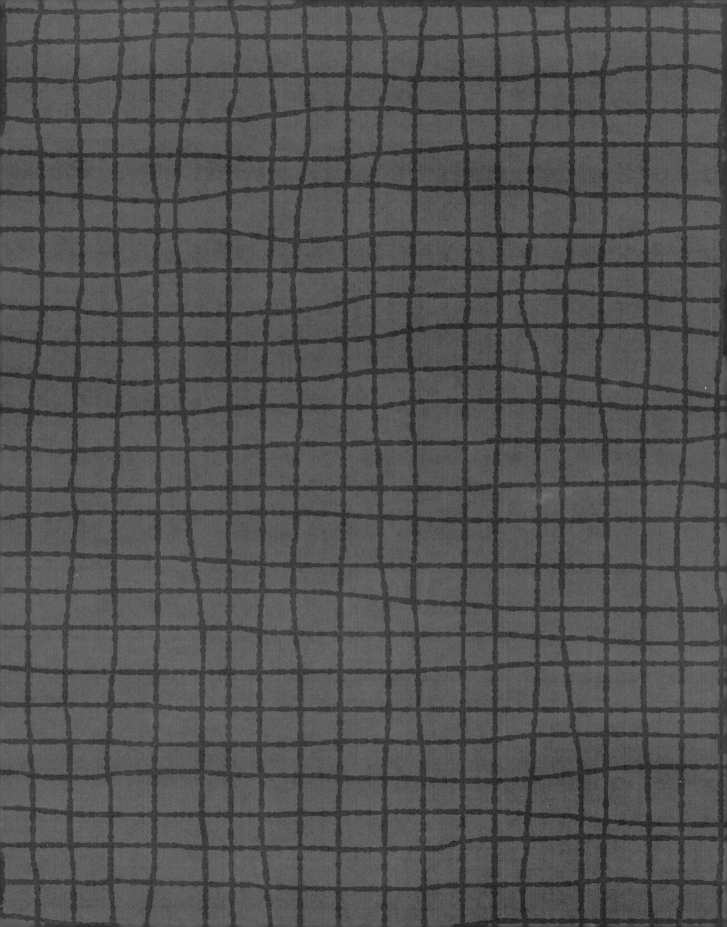

Guy Savoy 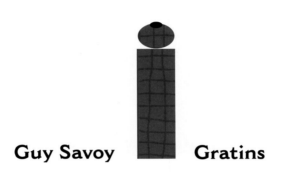 Gratins

# GRATIN DAUPHINOIS

2 pounds russet potatoes

2 tablespoons unsalted butter

2 garlic cloves

2 cups milk

1 cup heavy cream

Salt and freshly ground black pepper

Peel and rinse the potatoes and cut them into $\frac{1}{8}$-inch slices. Spread the slices in a 2-quart baking dish about 2 inches deep. Cut the butter into small pieces and scatter over the potatoes.

Preheat the oven to 350°F or 300°F, depending on the time you plan to cook the gratin.

Peel and mince the garlic cloves. Place them in a medium saucepan, along with the milk and cream and bring just to a boil. Turn off the heat and season with salt and pepper to taste. Strain the mixture over the potatoes and gently shake the pan to distribute the liquid evenly. Cover the baking dish with aluminum foil and poke a few holes with a knife to allow some steam to escape while it bakes. Bake for 1 hour at 350°F or 2 hours at 300°F. Check for doneness by inserting a small knife through the potatoes; they should be very soft.

Just before serving, remove the aluminum foil and place the gratin under the broiler until it turns a golden brown.

*Slow cooking is the secret to a perfect gratin dauphinois. Ideally the gratin should be cooked at a low temperature for two hours to allow the potatoes to gradually absorb the milk and cream and become soft. Here I also give you a faster option, but I encourage you to take your time with this recipe. This dish goes well with red meat or poultry dishes.*

# CAULIFLOWER
## AND SALT COD GRATIN

1 pound salt cod

Salt

1 medium head cauliflower

2½ cups heavy cream

Freshly ground black pepper

Soak the cod in cold water for 24 hours, changing the water every 5 to 6 hours.

Drain the cod. Trim the cauliflower and separate it into florets, discarding the stems.

Bring a large pot of salted water to a boil. Fill a large bowl with cold water and a handful of ice cubes. Blanch the cauliflower in the boiling water for 4 to 5 minutes. Drain and immediately place the cauliflower in the ice water. Drain again.

Preheat the oven to 350°F.

Reduce the cream by half in a small saucepan over medium-low heat. Lightly season with pepper. Discard any bones and skin from the cod and cut into 1¾-inch pieces.

Combine the cod and cauliflower in a 2-quart baking dish about 2 inches deep. Add the cream and bake for 20 minutes, or until golden. Serve immediately.

*This gratin can be served on its own as a main course. In this recipe, the cod is used both as an ingredient and a seasoning. Its pungent taste holds up to the relatively neutral flavor of the cauliflower. For a nice presentation, garnish with minced fresh herbs such as parsley, chervil, or chives just before serving.*

# SPINACH AND MUSHROOM
## GRATIN

1 pound spinach

1 pound white mushrooms

Salt

1½ tablespoons unsalted butter

1¼ cups heavy cream

Freshly ground black pepper

Cut off and discard any large spinach stems, then wash the spinach in cold water and drain. Cut the mushrooms into very thin slices. Heat the butter in a medium skillet over high heat, add the mushrooms, and sauté until golden. Drain in a colander and set aside.

Bring 2 quarts of salted water to a boil. Fill a large bowl with cold water and a handful of ice cubes. Blanch the spinach in the boiling water for 2 seconds, then drain and immediately place the spinach in the ice water. Drain again.

Preheat the oven to 350°F. Reduce the cream by two-thirds in a small saucepan over medium-low heat. Season with salt and pepper to taste.

Spread the spinach around the bottom of a small baking dish in an even layer. Arrange the mushroom slices over it in a fish scale pattern. Add the cream and bake for 5 minutes.

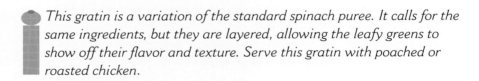

*This gratin is a variation of the standard spinach puree. It calls for the same ingredients, but they are layered, allowing the leafy greens to show off their flavor and texture. Serve this gratin with poached or roasted chicken.*

# SWISS CHARD
## GRATIN

Separate the chard leaves from stems. Reserve the leaves for another use. Trim the base of the stems and remove the fibrous strings. Rinse the stems under cold water and cut them into small sticks, about ½ inch by 2 inches. Bring a large pot of salted water to a boil. Add the lemon juice and chard and cook for 15 minutes. Drain.

Preheat the oven to 300°F. Combine the chicken stock and peppercorns in a small saucepan. Reduce by three-quarters over medium-low heat. Add the cream and bay leaf and reduce by two-thirds.

Spread the chard on a cookie sheet and place in the oven for 8 to 10 minutes to dry. The chard should not brown. Remove from the oven and raise the temperature to 350°F. Butter the bottom and sides of a small baking dish. Add the chard and sprinkle with salt to taste. Add the cream, stir well to combine, and bake for 5 to 6 minutes. Serve immediately.

2 pounds Swiss chard

Salt

Juice of 1 lemon

½ cup chicken stock (see recipe, page 136)

½ teaspoon black peppercorns

2½ cups heavy cream

1 bay leaf

*Memories of the Swiss chard gratins of my youth conjure up the flavors of bay. It is the only dish in which I allow the taste of the bay leaf to be obvious. The aroma of the herb blends perfectly with the slight acidity of the Swiss chard. Serve this gratin with a veal roast or an oven-roasted fish such as porgy or snapper. Don't forget to have a little bread on hand to dunk into the delicious bay leaf–scented sauce.*

# PUMPKIN
## GRATIN

Peel the pumpkin and remove the fibers and seeds. Cut the flesh into 1-inch cubes.

Melt the butter in a large pot, add the pumpkin cubes, and sprinkle with salt. Cover and cook, stirring occasionally, over medium-low heat for 40 minutes, or until the pumpkin is soft and the liquid has evaporated. Puree in a food processor. Transfer to a large bowl and stir in the cream and grated cheese, and season with salt and pepper to taste. Stir well and set aside.

Preheat the oven to 350°F.

Spread the pumpkin puree in a 2-quart baking dish in a 1½-inch layer. Bake for 15 minutes, or until golden. Serve immediately.

*In this recipe, it's important that all the moisture from the pumpkin evaporates and the pulp is dry, and that the puree is spread into a thin layer, no thicker than 1½ inches. This gratin can be served with roasted fowl or, in the winter, a game bird such as wild mallard.*

One 2-pound pumpkin

2 tablespoons unsalted butter

Salt

1 cup heavy cream

½ cup grated Parmesan or Gruyère cheese

Freshly ground black pepper

# MACARONI
## AND CHEESE

Salt

½ pound elbow macaroni

1¼ cups milk

2 cups heavy cream

1 cup grated Gruyère or
Emmental cheese

Freshly ground black pepper

The day before you plan to serve the gratin, bring a large pot of salted water to a boil. Add the macaroni and cook for 4 minutes, or until very al dente. Drain and cool under cold running water. In a mixing bowl, combine the milk, cream, and half of the cheese. Toss in the pasta and blend well. Season with salt and pepper to taste. Cover with plastic wrap and refrigerate for 24 hours. The pasta will absorb the milk mixture and expand.

When ready to serve, bring the pasta to room temperature. Preheat the oven to 400°F.

Place the pasta in a 2-quart baking dish. Sprinkle the remaining cheese on top. Bake for 15 to 20 minutes, or until golden and crusty. Serve immediately.

*Gratins made with pasta are part of some of the most memorable childhood moments, and among them, macaroni and cheese is king. Although very simple, the preparation of this gratin is spread out over two days. A great macaroni and cheese should be dry and crisp, and the layer of pasta should not be too thick.*

# PURPLE
## ARTICHOKE GRATIN

Juice of ½ lemon

20 small purple artichokes

¾ pound white mushrooms

1 shallot

2 tablespoons unsalted butter

1 cup heavy cream

2 tablespoons olive oil

2 sprigs thyme

Salt and freshly ground black pepper

½ cup veal stock (see recipe, page 137)

2 slices good-quality white bread

2 ounces Parmesan cheese

In a large mixing bowl, combine the lemon juice with 1 quart cold water. Set aside.

Cut off the stems of the artichokes leaving ½ inch at the base. Break off the dark green leaves until the pale tender ones are exposed. Using a sharp paring knife, trim all around the base as closely as possible without cutting or shaving the heart. Cut crosswise, removing the top two-thirds of the leaves. Carefully remove the chokes with a spoon. Place the artichoke hearts in the lemon water as you go along to avoid discoloration.

Trim the mushrooms and finely chop them. Mince the shallot. Heat the butter in a large pot over medium heat. Add the shallot and cook for 3 minutes, or until translucent. Add the mushrooms and cook for another 5 minutes, stirring constantly. Add the cream and cook until the liquid has evaporated. Remove from the heat and set aside.

Drain the artichoke hearts. Heat the olive oil in a large frying pan over medium heat. Add the artichoke hearts along with the thyme and sauté until they are lightly golden. Season with salt and pepper to taste. Lower the heat and cook for another 5 minutes. Add the veal stock and cook for another 5 minutes. The artichoke hearts should be soft and glazed with the veal stock.

Preheat the oven to 350°F.

Spread the mushrooms in an even layer about ¾-inch thick in a shallow baking dish large enough to hold the artichokes in a single layer. Place the artichokes on top, stem side up, and bake for 10 minutes. Meanwhile, cut the bread into ½-inch cubes and shave the Parmesan using a vegetable peeler.

Remove the gratin from the oven. Turn on the broiler. Sprinkle the bread and cheese over the gratin and broil for a few seconds, until just golden. Serve immediately.

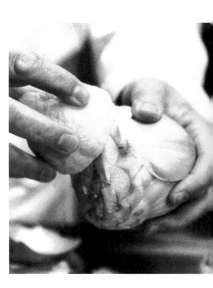

*This is a "dry" gratin, similar to roasted vegetables. You can serve it with a leg of lamb or a roasted poultry dish, or on its own as a light supper. The Parmesan should melt slightly, but don't let it burn.*

# PROVENÇAL
## GRATIN

2 medium onions

3 tablespoons olive oil

3 medium eggplants

3 medium zucchini

6 medium tomatoes

Salt and freshly ground
black pepper

4 sprigs thyme

Thinly slice the onions. Heat 1 tablespoon of the oil in a medium skillet over medium-low heat. Add the onions and cook, covered, for 20 minutes, or until very soft.

Preheat the oven to 350°F.

Thinly slice the eggplants, zucchini, and tomatoes.

Spread the onions around the bottom of a large baking dish. Arrange the vegetables over them in alternating rows of tomato, zucchini, and eggplant. Season with salt and pepper to taste. Sprinkle with the thyme and drizzle the remaining 2 tablespoons of the oil on top.

Bake 1 hour, until the vegetables have softened. Serve immediately.

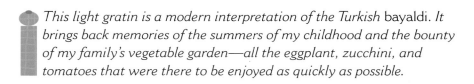

*This light gratin is a modern interpretation of the Turkish* bayaldi. *It brings back memories of the summers of my childhood and the bounty of my family's vegetable garden—all the eggplant, zucchini, and tomatoes that were there to be enjoyed as quickly as possible.*

# SAUSAGE AND POTATO
## GRATIN

4 medium potatoes

Salt

2 medium onions

1 small head Savoy cabbage

1 tablespoon unsalted butter

7 ounces beef marrow

1 pound andouille or
kielbasa sausage (see Note)

1 tablespoon vegetable oil

Freshly ground black pepper

Wash the potatoes and place them in a large pot of cold salted water. Bring to a boil and cook for 15 to 20 minutes, or until tender.

Thinly slice the onions. Trim and remove the tough outer leaves from the cabbage. Cut crosswise into ¼-inch strips.

Heat the butter in a large pot. Add the onions and cabbage. Season with salt and pepper to taste and cook, covered, over low heat for 15 minutes, or until the cabbage is wilted and tender.

Place the marrow in a saucepan and cover with cold water. Bring to a boil, remove from the heat, and drain. Drain and peel the potatoes.

Preheat the oven to 400°F.

Spread the cabbage and onion mixture in the bottom of a large baking dish, in an even layer about 1-inch thick. Cut the potatoes and sausage into ½-inch thick slices. Arrange over the cabbage alternating the slices of potatoes and sausage. Drizzle with the oil and bake for 10 minutes.

Remove from the oven and turn on the broiler. Cut the marrow into ¾-inch slices and arrange on top of the gratin. Broil for a few seconds, until golden, and serve immediately.

**Note:** In my home kitchen, I use a French andouille sausage for this recipe. Although, the French unsmoked chitterling sausage is milder than the Cajun andouille or the kielbasa, they share the same robust character. A good-quality, unsmoked garlic sausage can also be used for this recipe.

*Like the preceding recipe, this is a gratin to be served as a main course. It is rustic and rich, ideal for cold weather. Add the marrow at the last minute, making sure not to overcook it; it should not shrivel under the heat.*

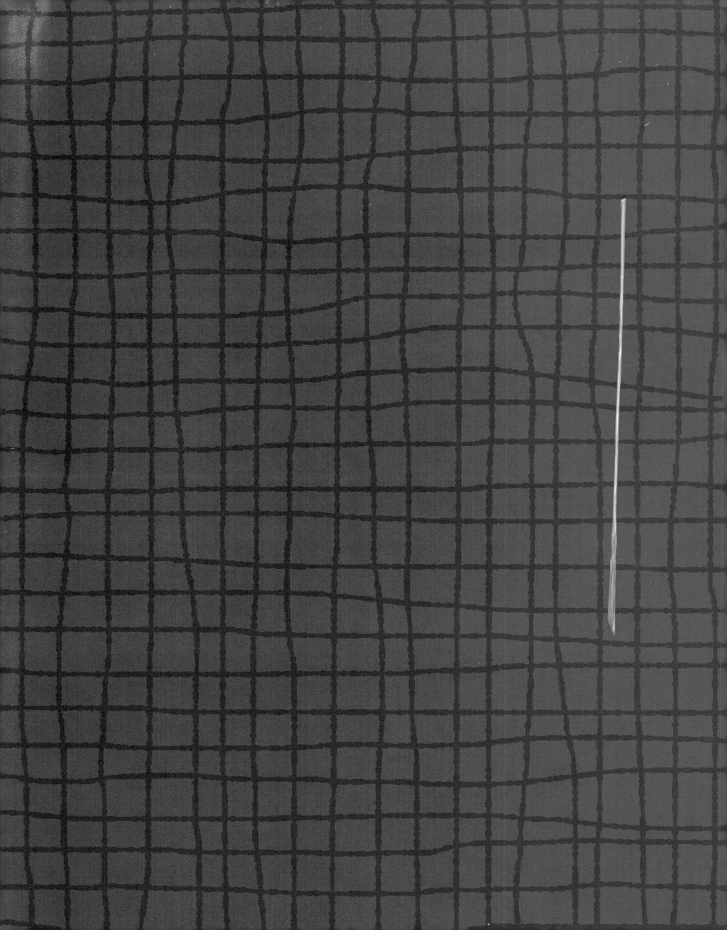

**Guy Savoy**     **Fish**

# MUSTARD ROASTED SKATE
## WITH LENTILS

1 medium onion

1 medium carrot

4 ounces green lentils

Salt

Bouquet garni (¼ bay leaf, 2 sprigs Italian parsley, 1 sprig thyme), tied in cheesecloth

4 skate wings, about 10 ounces each

12 tablespoons unsalted butter

Freshly ground black pepper

2 tablespoons Dijon mustard

Cut the onion and carrot into large chunks.

Rinse the lentils in cold water and place them in a large pot. Cover with cold water, season with salt, and bring to a boil. Skim off any foam that forms at the surface, and add the onion, carrot and bouquet garni. Lower the heat to medium, cover, and cook for 25 minutes, or until the lentils are soft.

Meanwhile, rinse the skate wings and dry them on paper towels.

Drain the lentils. Discard the bouquet garni and onion and carrot pieces. Return the lentils to the pot and set over low heat. Stir in 5 tablespoons of the butter, a few pieces at a time, until the mixture is creamy. Season to taste with salt and pepper. Keep warm.

Coat both sides of the skate wings with the mustard. Heat 2 tablespoons of the butter in a large skillet over medium heat. Add the skate wings and sauté for 5 minutes on each side, until golden. Remove from the pan and keep warm.

Pour off the fat from the pan. Add the remaining 5 tablespoons butter and cook over medium heat until the butter becomes hazelnut in color.

Spoon the lentils on 4 individual serving plates, arrange the skate wings on top, and drizzle the butter around the edges. Serve immediately.

*The mustard in this dish forms a golden shell around the fish and sears in the juices. Skate has an interesting texture and consistency, and sautéing it with the mustard accentuates its personality. You may add some minced parsley to the butter at the last minute.*

# ROASTED PORGY WITH
## "GREEK-STYLE" VEGETABLES

Peel the turnips, carrots, and zucchini and cut them into 2-inch sticks.

Bring a large pot of salted water to a boil. Blanch the turnips, carrots, zucchini, and cauliflower separately in the water, immediately plunging them in ice water to stop the cooking. Drain them, and then combine them in a large mixing bowl. Add the vinegar, coriander seeds, and ¾ cup of the olive oil. Stir until the vegetables are well coated with the dressing. Season with salt and pepper to taste. Cover with plastic wrap and refrigerate for at least 2 hours, or overnight. Remove from the refrigerator 30 minutes before serving.

Preheat the oven to 450°F.

Rinse and dry the porgy. Season with salt and pepper and stuff the cavities with the thyme. Place the porgy in a large baking dish and drizzle with the remaining ¼ cup olive oil. Roast for 10 minutes, basting regularly with the cooking juices.

Just before serving, halve the cherry tomatoes and toss them with the marinated vegetables. Spread the vegetable mixture on a large serving platter and arrange the porgy on top.

3 small turnips

3 medium carrots

3 medium zucchini

Salt

2 cups cauliflower florets

1¼ cups white wine vinegar

1 tablespoon whole
coriander seeds

1 cup extra-virgin olive oil

Freshly ground black pepper

2 small porgy, about 3
pounds each, cleaned and
scaled

6 sprigs thyme

½ pound cherry tomatoes

*Cooking the porgy whole is an excellent way to bring out the maximum flavor; it also highlights the complexity of this meaty, succulent fish. The vegetables should be served at room temperature—don't forget to take them out of the refrigerator at least a half hour before serving.*

# POACHED TURBOT
## WITH HOLLANDAISE SAUCE

14 tablespoons unsalted butter

2 pounds potatoes

Coarse salt

4 turbot fillets, about 4 ounces each (see Note)

1 quart milk

2 sprigs Italian parsley, plus additional for garnish

1 sprig thyme

¼ bay leaf

3 egg yolks

Salt and freshly ground black pepper

Juice of 1 lemon

Melt the butter in a small saucepan. Remove from the heat and let the milky residue settle to the bottom of the pan. Carefully pour the clear yellow liquid into a bowl, leaving behind the residue. Reserve the clarified butter.

Peel the potatoes and cut them into ½-inch slices. Place the potatoes in a large pot and cover with cold water. Season with coarse salt and bring to a boil. Lower the heat and simmer for 10 to 15 minutes, until the potato slices are cooked through but still firm.

Combine the milk, parsley, thyme, and bay leaf in a large saucepan. Bring to a boil, remove from the heat, and set aside to let the herbs infuse the milk.

Meanwhile, prepare the Hollandaise sauce. In a small saucepan, whisk the egg yolks with 1 tablespoon cold water until the mixture becomes frothy. Place the pan over low heat and cook, whisking constantly, for about 5 minutes, or until the mixture thickens, making sure the eggs don't curdle. When the mixture starts to thicken, remove from the heat and season with salt and pepper to taste. Slowly whisk in the melted butter. Stir in the lemon juice. Keep warm in a bain-marie or a mixing bowl set over hot water.

Rinse and dry the turbot fillets. Return the milk to the stove, bring to a simmer, and poach the fillets for 5 to 6 minutes. Carefully remove from the pan and drain on paper towels.

Arrange the fish and potatoes on a large serving platter. Sprinkle with parsley and serve with the Hollandaise sauce on the side.

*This is a classic recipe, perfect for special occasions. I strongly recommend that you use wild turbot instead of farm raised—flavor has a price! For the Hollandaise, adding water to the egg yolks helps with emulsifying. Make sure the egg yolks are very frothy before placing them on the stove and adding the butter. If you are unsure of yourself, use a bain-marie. And if the cooking time for the fish is too short for your taste, turn off the heat and leave the fillets in the hot milk for 2 to 3 minutes.*

**Note:** Turbot is a mild white fish that is sold frozen in better fish markets. If it's not available, substitute with halibut or striped bass fillets.

Preparation Time: **15 minutes**
Cooking Time: **10 minutes**

# SOLE GOUJONNETTES
## WITH BROCCOLI PUREE

1 pound broccoli

¼ cup extra-virgin olive oil

Salt and freshly ground black pepper

4 gray sole fillets, about 6 ounces each

2 tablespoons unsalted butter

Trim and cut the broccoli into florets. Peel the stems and cut them into ½-inch pieces. Bring a large pot of salted water to a boil and blanch the broccoli florets and stems for 4 to 5 minutes. Immediately plunge the broccoli in ice water and drain.

Set aside 8 broccoli florets for garnish and place the rest of the florets and stems in the bowl of a food processor. Puree, adding the olive oil in a steady stream and salt and pepper to taste.

To make the sole goujonnettes, wash and dry the sole fillets. Cut them into strips about ½-inch wide. Lightly season with salt and pepper. Heat the butter in a large frying pan and sauté the sole over high heat for 30 seconds on each side.

Spoon the broccoli puree in the center of 4 individual serving plates. Arrange a few goujonnettes over it. Garnish with the reserved florets and serve immediately.

 *This dish can be served as a first course or a light entrée. You can also serve goujonnettes with a lemon and olive oil vinaigrette on the side. Make sure to cook the sole quickly over high heat.*

# SOLE MEUNIÈRE

4 sprigs Italian parsley

4 whole Dover soles, about 1 pound each (see Note)

2 lemons

¾ cup all-purpose flour

Salt and freshly ground black pepper

8 tablespoons unsalted butter

¼ cup grapeseed or vegetable oil

Mince the parsley and set aside.

Rinse the sole under cold running water and dry with paper towels.

Squeeze the lemons and strain the juice. Set aside.

Place the flour on a flat plate and season with salt and pepper to taste. Dredge the sole in the flour on both sides, shaking off any excess flour.

Heat 3 tablespoons of the butter with the grapeseed oil in a large frying pan over medium heat. Add the soles skin side down and cook for 3 to 4 minutes on each side, or until golden. Remove from the pan and keep warm.

Add the remaining 5 tablespoons butter to the pan. When the butter starts to bubble, add the parsley and lemon juice, swirling to combine. Season with salt and pepper to taste and pour over the soles. Serve immediately.

*Sole meunière is a real treat. For this recipe, I usually prefer the larger Dover soles that yield two servings each. I find them meatier and more satisfying than smaller ones. But don't worry if you can only find small ones at your local fish market—the dish will still be delicious. Make sure that the pocket of blood next to the head has been removed.*

**Note:** Frozen Dover soles can be purchased at better fish markets. If they're not available you can substitute lemon sole.

# WHITING EN PAPILLOTE
## WITH VEGETABLE SPAGHETTI

Peel and trim the carrots and turnips and cut them into a fine julienne. Peel the zucchini, reserving the flesh for another use. Cut the skin into a fine julienne.

Trim the leek. Insert a sharp paring knife about 2 inches above the root and cut through the entire length of the leek. Repeat until finely shredded. Wash well and dry with paper towels. Cut the leeks crosswise into 2-inch pieces.

Heat 2 tablespoons of the butter in a large skillet over medium-high heat, add the julienned carrots and turnip, and cook for 5 minutes. Add the zucchini skins and leek, season with salt and pepper to taste, cover, and cook for 5 minutes more; set aside.

Preheat the oven to 450°F. Rinse the whiting fillets and dry them on paper towels. Melt the remaining 2 tablespoons butter in a small saucepan.

Cut four 15-inch squares of aluminum foil. Brush some of the melted butter on half of each square. Place a whiting fillet at the center of each buttered half. Season with salt and pepper. Arrange the julienned vegetables over the fillets, squeeze some lemon juice over them, and garnish each with a sprig of thyme. Fold the unbuttered side of the foil over the fish and vegetables and fold down the edges to make a tight package.

Place the papillotes on a large baking sheet and bake for 7 minutes. Serve immediately.

2 large carrots

2 turnips

2 large zucchini

1 medium leek

4 tablespoons unsalted butter

Salt and freshly ground black pepper

4 whiting fillets, about 6 ounces each

4 sprigs fresh thyme

Juice of 1 lemon

*Please note that whiting has a delicate flesh and requires an exact cooking time. I must insist that this cooking time be respected and that the papillote be opened as soon as it is removed from the oven. Otherwise the fish will keep cooking and the dish will be ruined.*

# YELLOW PERCH IN RED
## WINE SAUCE WITH LEEK

5 large leeks

10 tablespoons unsalted butter

Salt

1 cup sliced shallots

1½ cups red wine

Freshly ground black pepper

1 slice prosciutto, about 2 ounces each

4 yellow perch fillets, about 6 ounces each

4 sprigs chervil

Cut off the top green part of the leeks. Remove the roots and any blemished outer leaves. Insert a sharp paring knife about 2 inches above the root and cut through the entire length of the leeks. Wash well and dry with paper towels. Cut the leeks crosswise into ½-inch slices. Heat 2 tablespoons of the butter in a large pot over medium-low heat. Stir in the leeks, season with salt, cover, and cook for 20 minutes, or until the leeks are wilted and soft. Make sure the leeks do not brown.

Combine the shallots and wine in a small saucepan over medium heat and reduce by one-third, about 10 minutes. Bring to a boiland then remove from the heat. Whisk in 6 tablespoons of the butter, a few pieces at a time, until the sauce is thick and glistening. Season with salt and pepper and keep warm in a bain-marie or in a mixing bowl set over hot water. Cut the prosciutto into thin strips. Set aside.

Rinse and dry the fish. Season with salt and pepper on both sides. Heat the remaining 2 tablespoons butter in a large sauté pan. Add the fillets skin side down and cook for 5 minutes, then turn and cook for 3 additional minutes. Just before serving, stir half of the prosciutto strips into the leeks and divide the mixture among 4 serving plates. Place the fish on top and drizzle the red wine sauce around it. Garnish with the chervil and remaining ham.

*The red wine sauce enhances the flavor of yellow perch, a river fish with an interesting texture but subtle taste. The addition of the ham further emphasizes the flavors. This autumn dish is a tribute to my friend Bernard Loiseau, an accomplice during my apprenticing years, and simply an accomplice in life.*

# BRILL WITH CRUSHED
## POTATOES AND TAPENADE

2 garlic cloves

¾ pound potatoes

2 sprigs thyme

Salt

1 cup extra-virgin olive oil

8 ounces pitted black olives

2 ounces canned anchovies, drained

Freshly ground black pepper

8 brill fillets, about 3 ounces each

Preheat the oven to 350°F.

Peel the garlic cloves and halve them. Then peel the potatoes and cut them into a small dice. Rinse under cold running water. Drain and dry on paper towels. Spread the potatoes in an even layer, about 1½-inches thick, in a large baking dish. Add the garlic and thyme. Season with salt. Drizzle with 2 tablespoons of the olive oil and ½ cup of water. Cover the dish with aluminum foil and bake for 40 minutes.

To make the tapenade, place the olives and anchovies in the bowl of a food processor. Lightly season with pepper and coarsely chop. Add 4 tablespoons of the oil and puree until smooth and creamy. Adjust the seasonings, pour into a bowl, and set aside.

Remove the garlic and thyme from the potatoes. Mash the potatoes with a fork to a fine texture.

Rinse and dry the fish. Season with salt and pepper to taste. Heat the remaining 10 tablespoons oil in a nonstick skillet over high heat. Cook the fillets for 2 minutes on each side.

Divide the potatoes among 4 individual serving plates and cover with two brill fillets each. Drizzle the tapenade on top and around the fish. Serve immediately.

*I love brill! It is a fish too often forgotten, and when you cook with brill, as an added bonus you always know you are buying a wild fish. Its texture and flavor are excellent, and here they are nicely accentuated by the tapenade. You can flavor the potatoes with minced fresh herbs such as sage, chervil, and chives.*

# POACHED TROUT "AU BLEU"

2 medium carrots

1 medium onion

Bouquet garni (¼ bay leaf, 2 sprigs parsley, 1 sprig thyme), tied in cheesecloth

1 tablespoon coarse sea salt

1¼ cups white wine vinegar

4 whole trout, cleaned and scaled, about 6 ounces each

Salt and freshly ground black pepper

Cut the carrots and onions into large chunks.

To make a court-bouillon, fill a large pot with 6 cups of water over high heat. Add the carrots, onion, bouquet garni, coarse salt, and ½ cup of the vinegar. Bring to a boil, lower the heat, and simmer for 20 minutes.

While you're making the court-boullion, place the trout on a platter and baste frequently with the remaining ¾ cups vinegar.

Reduce the heat under the court-bouillon to a very low simmer and poach the trout for 6 to 8 minutes. Carefully remove from the broth with a slotted spoon and place on a serving platter. Serve with steamed potatoes. Season with salt and pepper to taste.

*For this family recipe the trout must be very fresh. Ideally they should be purchased alive, in which case you would hit them on the head before gutting them. Long ago, restaurant patrons ordered trout "au bleu" over the meunière style as a guarantee of freshness. Indeed, a trout that is not extremely fresh doesn't turn blue. The color comes from a chemical reaction with the vinegar. To ensure this reaction, it is best not to rinse or wipe the fish before cooking.*

Preparation Time: **20 minutes**
Cooking Time: **55 minutes**

# COD WITH BRAISED CARROTS
## AND THYME

Cut the carrots into thin slices. Peel and halve the garlic.

Heat ½ cup of the olive oil in a large nonstick skillet over medium heat. Add the carrots and garlic and cook, stirring frequently, until the carrots start to turn golden. Reduce the heat, season with salt, and cook, stirring occasionally, for 45 minutes, or until the carrots are very soft.

Rinse the fish and dry on paper towels. Slash the skin once with a sharp knife. Refrigerate until ready to cook.

Stir in the thyme with the carrots. Remove the pan from the heat, discard the garlic, cover, and set aside.

Heat the remaining ½ cup olive oil in a large nonstick skillet. Season the cod with salt and pepper to taste. Add the cod, skin side down, and cook over medium heat for 4 to 5 minutes. Turn and cook for another 4 to 5 minutes.

Divide the carrots among 4 individual serving plates, place a cod fillet on top of each, and garnish with a few drops of olive oil and a sprig of thyme.

2 pounds medium carrots

1 garlic clove

1 cup extra-virgin olive oil, plus more for serving

4 cod fillets with the skins, about 6 ounces each

4 sprigs fresh thyme, plus more for garnish

Salt and freshly ground black pepper

*Cod is becoming more and more rare. Bought at its freshest, it is translucent, crystalline, and delicious. Here its delicate texture works with the sweet carrots and is enhanced by the strong flavors of the thyme and olive oil.*

# FISH STOCK

1 pound fish bones, preferably sole or any other lean fish

1 medium onion

1 sprig thyme

2 sprigs Italian parsley

Place the fish bones in a colander in the sink and set under running water for 15 minutes. Thinly slice the onion. Place the fish bones in a stockpot and cover with 2 quarts of cold water over high heat. Bring to a boil, skimming off any foam that rises to the surface. Add the onion, thyme, and parsley. Lower the heat and simmer for 10 minutes. Strain through a chinois or fine-mesh strainer and allow to cool.

*It is always best to make a fish stock using the bones from the same fish you are using in a recipe. It will help preserve the integrity of the ingredients and the dish. Sometimes, mussel juice can be added to enhance the flavor of the fish stock. Fish stock will keep for up to three days in the refrigerator, or it may be frozen in ice cube trays and stored in the freezer in small plastic bags.*

**Guy Savoy**     **Meat**

# STEAK TARTARE

1 large onion

5 cornichons

1 tablespoon capers

2 sprigs Italian parsley

1¼ pounds sirloin steak, preferably organic and grass-fed

4 very fresh organic egg yolks

Tabasco Sauce to taste

Ketchup to taste

Fleur de sel and freshly ground pepper

Finely mince the onion. Separately mince the cornichons, capers, and parsley. Place them in small serving bowls and set aside.

Using a very sharp knife, trim the sirloin, removing as much fat as possible. Cut the meat into ¼-inch dice.

Divide the meat among 4 individual serving plates. Shape the meat into a dome, make an indentation in the center, and nestle the egg yolks in it.

Serve with the onions, capers, cornichons, parsley, Tabasco, ketchup, fleur de sel, and pepper on the side for each guest to season the tartare according to their taste. Serve with a green salad.

When I'm stuck and can't come up with anything to prepare for a meal at home, I often turn to the reliable steak tartare. This is a dish that is both simple and elaborate. It holds a lot of ingredients but doesn't require cooking. The only thing to be careful about is the quality of the ingredients. During the summer months, I like to prepare it in a salad bowl set over ice.

Preparation Time: **30 minutes**

Cooking Time: **45 minutes**

# VEAL KIDNEYS IN MUSTARD
## SAUCE WITH MASHED POTATOES

2 pounds potatoes

1 tablespoon coarse salt

1¼ cups milk

12 tablespoons unsalted butter

12 ounces veal kidneys, trimmed

2 tablespoons grapeseed or vegetable oil

3 ounces old-fashioned grainy mustard

1 cup veal stock (see recipe page 137)

Salt and freshly ground pepper

Place the potatoes in a large pot and cover with cold water. Add the coarse salt and bring to a boil over high heat. Lower the heat and cook for 25 to 30 minutes, or until soft. Meanwhile, bring the milk just to a boil in a small saucepan over medium heat. Remove from the heat and set aside.

Drain the potatoes and peel them while still hot. Pass the potatoes through a food mill, and then stir in the milk. Return the mashed potatoes to the pot over low heat. Beat in 8 tablespoons of the butter until creamy and smooth. Season with salt and keep warm.

Cut the kidneys in ¾-inch slices. Heat 2 tablespoons of the butter and the oil in a large skillet over high heat. Sear the kidney slices for 30 seconds on each side. They must remain pink. Remove to a plate or a rack to drain.

Deglaze the pan with 1½ ounces of the mustard and the stock. Reduce over medium heat by one-third. Swirl in the remaining 2 tablespoons butter. Season with salt and pepper. Keep warm.

Fold the remaining 1½ ounces mustard into the mashed potatoes and slowly reheat them. Divide the kidney slices among 4 individual serving plates. Spoon the mashed potatoes around them and drizzle with the sauce.

*Mustard pairs well with veal kidneys, and by adding some mustard to the mashed potatoes, I also use the side dish as a seasoning. I lament the disappearance of offal shops, but don't resign yourself to this fate— if you can't find kidneys, sweetbreads, or heart at your butcher shop, don't hesitate to order them.*

# BRAISED PORK
## WITH CHESTNUTS

Quarter the mushrooms and set aside. Preheat the oven to 375°F. Season the pork with salt and pepper on both sides. Heat 4 tablespoons of the butter in a large pot over medium heat. Sauté the pork until golden on both sides. Add the water, cover, and bake in the oven for 20 minutes. Add the stock, season with salt and pepper, return to the oven, and bake for another 45 minutes.

Add the chestnuts and mushrooms to the pot. Cover and bake for 45 minutes, or until the meat is very tender. Remove the meat from the pot and place on a serving platter.

Skim off as much fat as possible from the top of the cooking juices. Swirl in the remaining 4 tablespoons butter and let the sauce reduce slightly on the stove over medium-low heat. Season with salt and pepper to taste. Arrange the chestnuts and mushrooms around the meat and spoon the sauce over them. Serve immediately.

*This braised pork reminds me of my childhood. When I got back from school, I would always be happy to find out we were having it for dinner. With its slightly caramelized chestnuts and thick juices, this is the quintessential autumn dish. By all means, you can substitute wild mushrooms for the white ones—a few sautéed cèpes, for example, couldn't hurt.*

10 ounces white mushrooms

One 2-pound slice fresh ham, preferably from the shank

Salt and freshly ground black pepper

8 tablespoons unsalted butter

½ cup water

1 cup veal stock (see recipe, page 137)

One 10-ounce can chestnuts packed in water

# BEEF STEW WITH CARROTS

2 medium onions

1 celery rib

10 medium carrots

One 2-pound beef brisket

Salt and freshly ground black pepper

3 tablespoons unsalted butter

2 tablespoons all-purpose flour

5 cups red wine

4 cups veal stock (see recipe, page 137)

Bouquet garni (¼ bay leaf, 2 sprigs parsley, 1 sprig thyme), tied in cheesecloth

3 garlic cloves, peeled and crushed

1 tablespoon tomato paste

1 tablespoon minced parsley

Cut the onions, celery, and 2 of the carrots into large chunks. Sprinkle the brisket with salt and pepper on both sides.

Heat the butter in a deep skillet over medium-high heat. Sear the beef until golden brown on both sides. Add the onion, carrot, and celery chunks and sprinkle with the flour. Stir well to coat the meat and vegetables evenly. Add the red wine and cook for 2 to 3 minutes over high heat, scraping the bottom of the pan.

Transfer the meat and vegetables to a large heavy pot. Add the veal stock, bouquet garni, garlic, and tomato paste. Season with salt and pepper to taste. Cover and cook for 1 hour and 20 minutes over low heat.

Meanwhile, cut the remaining 8 carrots into ¼-inch slices. Add them to the pot and cook for another 30 to 40 minutes, or until meat is tender and the carrots are soft but still hold their shape.

Remove the meat from the pot and place it on a cutting board. Remove the carrot slices and keep them warm. Strain the sauce and return it to the pot. Adjust the seasonings. If the sauce seems too thin, reduce slightly until syrupy.

Cut the meat into ½-inch slices and arrange on a serving platter. Spoon the sauce over it and scatter the carrots around. Sprinkle with the minced parsley and serve immediately.

*Like most braised dishes, this winter classic is very simple to prepare. It is sad to witness the technique of braising slowly disappear from the culinary repertoire of the home cook. Don't be intimidated by long the cooking time. Preparing a beef stew with carrots is less complicated than a sole meunière—all you have to do is let it cook.*

Preparation Time: **30 minutes**
Cooking Time: **2½ hours**

# CHICKEN IN A POT
## WITH BASMATI RICE

**For the chicken:**

1 medium onion

2 large carrots

1 celery rib

2 large turnips

1 medium leek

1 whole 4-pound hen
(see Note)

2 tablespoons coarse salt

10 white peppercorns

Bouquet garni (¼ bay leaf,
2 sprigs parsley, 1 sprig
thyme), tied in cheesecloth

2½ cups heavy cream

3 egg yolks

Salt and freshly ground
black pepper

**For the rice:**

1½ cups chicken broth
(see recipe, page 136)

1 medium onion

4 tablespoons unsalted
butter

8 ounces basmati rice

Salt and freshly ground
black pepper

**Make the chicken:** Peel the onions, carrots, celery, and turnips. Trim the leek. Insert a sharp paring knife about 2 inches above the root and cut through the entire length of the leek. Wash well and dry with paper towels.

Rinse the hen under cold running water and place it in a large stockpot. Cover with cold water and bring to a boil. Cook for 5 minutes, skimming off any foam rising to the surface. Add the onion, celery, coarse salt, peppercorns, and bouquet garni. Bring back to a boil, lower the heat, and simmer for 1½ hours. Add the leek, carrots, and turnips and cook for another 30 minutes.

Preheat the oven to 400°F.

**Make the rice:** Bring the chicken stock to a boil in a small saucepan over medium heat. Remove from the heat and set aside. Mince the onion. Heat 1½ tablespoons of the butter in an ovenproof saucepan over medium heat. Cook the onion until translucent, about 1 minute. Do not brown. Stir in the rice with a wooden spoon until well coated with butter. Add the hot broth and season with salt and pepper to taste. Turn the heat to high and bring to a boil. Cover the saucepan and place in the oven. Bake for 15 minutes. The rice should remain slightly crunchy.

Cut the remaining 2½ tablespoons butter into small pieces and dot the rice with it. Cover and set aside.

Remove the hen from the broth and set aside in a warm place. Strain the broth into a large saucepan, reserving the vegetables. Reduce the broth by half over high heat. Add the cream and reduce for few more minutes, until the mixture becomes thick and coats the back of a spoon. Remove from the heat and cool for a few minutes. Whisk in the egg yolks, one at the time. Season with salt and pepper to taste.

Cut the hen into serving pieces and transfer to a serving platter with the reserved vegetables. Fluff up the rice with a spoon and place in a serving bowl. Spoon some of the sauce over the meat and vegetables and serve the remainder in a sauceboat.

*This is a good example of a delicious dish made with inexpensive ingredients. The nutty flavors of the basmati rice and the complexity of the rich broth deliver a dish that is very savory and healthy providing that most of the fat is removed from the broth.*

**Note:** You may use a 4-pound chicken instead of a hen. If you're using a chicken, cooking time should be reduced to 45 minutes and all of the vegetables should be added to the pot with the chicken.

Preparation Time: **20 minutes**
Cooking Time: **1½ hours**

# ROASTED CHICKEN
## WITH MASHED POTATOES

1 whole 3½-pound free-range chicken, neck and wing tips reserved

Coarse salt

½ teaspoon freshly ground black pepper

4 sprigs thyme

¼ bay leaf

1 garlic clove, peeled

4 tablespoons grapeseed or vegetable oil

1 medium onion, quartered

16 tablespoons unsalted butter

1¼ pounds potatoes

¾ cup milk

Salt and freshly ground black pepper

Preheat the oven to 400°F.

Rinse and dry the chicken. Sprinkle the cavity with 1 teaspoon coarse salt and ground pepper and stuff with the thyme, bay leaf, and garlic. Place the chicken in a roasting pan. Season with salt and pepper and drizzle with the oil. Place the onion around the chicken. Cut 4 tablespoons of the butter into small pieces and scatter them around the chicken. Roast for 1 hour, basting regularly with the cooking juices. The skin should be crisp and golden.

Meanwhile, place the potatoes in a large pot and cover with cold water. Add coarse salt and bring to a boil. Lower the heat and cook for 25 to 30 minutes, or until cooked through. Meanwhile, bring the milk to a boil. Remove from the heat and set aside.

Drain the potatoes and peel them while still hot. Pass them through a food mill. Stir in the milk. Return the mashed potatoes to the pot over low heat and beat in the remaining 12 tablespooons butter until creamy and smooth. Season with salt and set aside in a warm place.

Remove the chicken from the oven and place it on a cutting board. Keep warm. Deglaze the roasting pan with 1 cup of water, scraping the bottom of the pan. Pour the juices into a saucepan and reduce by one-quarter. Season with salt and pepper to taste and strain. Cut the chicken into serving pieces and transfer to a platter. Serve with the mashed potatoes and sauce on the side.

*In my childhood home, as soon as the chicken came out of the oven, in went the apple tart. The memory of these combined aromas are symbolic of the cozy atmosphere of the home. To get the full effect we should all turn off the exhaust fan once a week to enjoy the fragrant smells of a roasted chicken logically followed by those of an apple tart. (See Apple Tart recipe, page 162.)*

Preparation Time: **40 minutes**
+ **24 hours for chilling**

Cooking Time: **1 hour**

# RABBIT STEW
## WITH CREAMY POLENTA

1 medium carrot

1 medium onion

One 4- to 5-pound roaster rabbit (see Note)

1 sprig thyme

½ bay leaf

2 quarts red wine

½ cup extra-virgin olive oil

3 tablespoons unsalted butter

3 tablespoons all-purpose flour

2 garlic cloves, peeled and crushed

Bouquet garni (¼ bay leaf, 2 sprigs parsley, 1 sprig thyme), tied in cheesecloth

Salt and freshly ground black pepper

For the polenta:

3½ cups milk

2½ cups heavy cream

1 cup instant polenta

6 tablespoons unsalted butter

Salt and freshly ground black pepper

Bread cubes sautéed in butter and sprinkled with parsley (optional)

Ask your butcher to cut the rabbit into serving pieces. Reserve the liver.

Peel the carrot and onion and chop coarsely. Place the rabbit pieces with the carrot, onion, thyme, and bay leaf in a large mixing bowl. Add the wine, stir well to combine, and cover the bowl with plastic wrap. Refrigerate for 24 hours. When ready to cook, remove the rabbit pieces from the marinade and set aside. Drain the marinade and reserve the vegetables and liquid separately.

Heat the oil and butter in a large skillet over medium-high heat. Sear the rabbit pieces on both sides until golden. Add the carrot and onion pieces from the marinade and sauté briefly. Sprinkle with the flour and stir well for 1 to 2 minutes to coat the meat and vegetables evenly. Transfer the meat and vegetables to a large pot and add the garlic cloves and bouquet garni. Pour in the reserved marinade and season with salt and pepper to taste. Bring to a boil, cover, then lower the heat and simmer for 45 minutes to 1 hour, or until the meat is tender.

To make the creamy polenta, combine the milk and cream in a large saucepan and bring to a boil. Reserve 1 cup of the mixture. Add the polenta to the remaining cream and milk, lower the heat to medium, and cook, stirring constantly for 10 to 15 minutes, or until the polenta starts pulling away from the sides of the pan. Remove from the heat.

Melt the butter over medium heat until it turns a hazelnut color. Stir it into the polenta and set aside.

Puree the rabbit liver in a food processor to a smooth consistency and pour it into a mixing bowl. Remove the rabbit pieces and vegetables from the pot with a slotted spoon and place in a deep serving dish. Keep warm.

Slowly add 1 cup of the cooking liquid to the pureed liver, stirring constantly, making sure it does not curdle. Stir the mixture back into the pot and simmer, whisking constantly for 1 minute, or until the sauce starts to thicken. Season with salt and pepper to taste, and strain the sauce over the rabbit and vegetables. Reheat the polenta, adding a little of the reserved milk mixture if it looks too thick. Pour into a serving bowl and serve with the rabbit. Serve with the sautéed bread cubes if desired.

*Italy is close to my native Dauphiné. Polenta is enjoyed there just as it is in the French Alps. It is a very versatile grain—you can serve it creamy, sautéed, fried, toasted. Here I use instant polenta as a time-saver. The liver is used as a binder to thicken the sauce and make it more flavorful.*

**Note:** Roaster rabbits are larger and meatier than the fryer grade and are perfect for stews. Roaster rabbits are available in better butcher shops or can be ordered from D'Artagnan. (800-DARTAGN; dartagnan.com).

# CHICKEN
## SHEPHERD'S PIE

1¼ pounds potatoes

1 tablespoon coarse salt

2 medium onions

1 pound cooked chicken meat

1 cup (16 tablespoons) unsalted butter

1 sprig thyme

Salt and freshly ground black pepper

¾ cup chicken stock (see recipe, page 136)

5 medium tomatoes

¾ cup milk

3 tablespoons breadcrumbs

2 sprigs parsley, minced

Place the potatoes in a large pot and cover with cold water. Add 1 tablespoon of coarse salt and bring to a boil. Lower the heat and cook for 25 to 30 minutes, or until cooked through.

Mince the onions and set aside. Coarsely chop the chicken meat and set aside.

Heat 2 tablespoons of the butter in a large skillet over medium heat and sauté the onions until translucent. Do not brown. Add the chicken and thyme. Season with salt and pepper to taste and cook for 2 to 3 minutes. Add the chicken stock, cover, and cook for 20 minutes over low heat.

Score the tomatoes with a sharp knife and plunge them in a pot of boiling water for 2 to 3 seconds. Remove from the water and cool. Peel and seed the tomatoes and cut the flesh into small dice. Add to the chicken and simmer for 5 minutes. Remove from the heat and set aside.

Bring the milk to a boil. Drain the potatoes and peel them while still hot. Pass through a food mill into a large bowl. Stir in the hot milk. Return the mashed potatoes to the pot over low heat and beat in the remaining 14 tablespoons butter until creamy and smooth. Season with salt to taste and set aside in a warm place.

Preheat the oven to 350°F.

Lightly butter a 1-quart baking dish. Spread a layer of the mashed potatoes over the bottom. Cover with a layer of the chicken mixture and continue filling the dish, alternating layers of potatoes and chicken. Finish with a layer of mashed potatoes. Sprinkle the top with the breadcrumbs and parsley and bake for 20 minutes. Serve immediately accompanied with a green salad.

*This recipe is a logical follow-up to the previous ones, as it is the combination of two classics: chicken in a pot and beef shepherd's pie.*

# LAMB CHOPS
## CHAMPVALLON-STYLE

2 pounds potatoes

3 medium onions

8 tablespoons unsalted butter

8 lamb chops

Salt and freshly ground black pepper

3 sprigs thyme

¼ bay leaf

4 cups veal stock (see recipe, page 137)

Peel the onions and potatoes and very thinly slice them.

Heat 4 tablespoons of the butter in a large skillet over medium heat. Add the onions and cook until soft and translucent. Do not brown. Remove from the skillet with a slotted spoon and set aside. Add the remaining 4 tablespoons butter to the skillet and sauté the potatoes until golden but still raw. Remove from the pan with a slotted spoon and set aside.

In the same skillet, brown the lamb chops on both sides over medium-high heat. Remove from the pan and season with salt and pepper.

Preheat the oven to 350°F. Layer the lamb chops in a large baking dish. Cover the chops with a layer of onions. Add the potatoes slices, making sure the meat is completely covered. Slide the thyme and bay leaf in between the layers.

Bring the veal stock to a boil in a medium saucepan and pour over the dish. Lightly season with salt and pepper. Bake for 1½ hours, or until the potatoes are very soft and the cooking liquid is reduced by half. Serve immediately.

*This great classic recipe dating back to the seventeenth century deserves to be rediscovered. It's at the crossroads of several culinary genres—classic cooking, home cooking, bourgeois cooking, and bistro cooking.*

# VEAL TONGUE
## WITH TARTAR SAUCE

Cut the carrots and onion into large chunks. Trim the leek. Insert a sharp paring knife about 2 inches above the root and cut through the entire length of the leek. Wash and dry with paper towels. Cut into large chunks.

Place the veal tongue in a large stockpot. Cover with cold water and bring to a boil. Cook for 5 minutes, skimming off any foam that rises to the surface. Add the carrots, onion, leek, bouquet garni, and coarse salt. Place a towel or cheesecloth folded in several layers on top of the water to keep the tongue immersed in the liquid. Lower the heat and simmer for 2 hours, or until the tip of a knife inserted in the thickest part of the tongue encounters no resistance.

Meanwhile, prepare the mayonnaise for the tartar sauce by combining the egg yolks, mustard, salt, and pepper in a medium mixing bowl. Add the oil in a steady stream, whisking vigorously until the mixture is thick and firm. Stir in the vinegar and adjust the seasonings. Refrigerate until ready to use.

Remove the tongue from the broth. Peel off the skin and cut away the gristle, tiny bones, and fat. Cut into 1/4-inch slices. Arrange the tongue slices on a serving dish. Stir the capers, cornichons, parsley, and chervil into the mayonnaise and serve with the tongue.

2 medium carrots

1 medium onion

1 medium leek

One 2-pound veal tongue

Bouquet garni ( 1/4 bay leaf, 2 sprigs parsley, 1 sprig thyme), tied in cheesecloth

1 tablespoon coarse salt

For the Tartar Sauce:

**2 very fresh organic egg yolks**

**2 teaspoons Dijon mustard**

**Salt and freshly ground black pepper**

**1 1/2 cups grapeseed or vegetable oil**

**1 teaspoon red wine vinegar**

**1 tablespoon chopped capers**

**1 tablespoon chopped cornichons**

**1 tablespoon minced parsley**

**1 tablespoon minced chervil**

*Tongue is an ingredient we rarely think about, but it's simple to cook with, easy to slice, and leaves behind very little waste. Since it has been largely forgotten, serving tongue at a dinner party will show some creativity on your part. This dish goes well with steamed potatoes or other vegetables such as carrots, turnips, or leeks.*

# STUFFED TOMATOES

2 medium carrots

1 medium onion

One 3-pound hen (see Note)

One ½-pound veal shank

¾ pound beef short ribs

Bouquet garni (¼ bay leaf, 2 sprigs parsley, 1 sprig thyme), tied in cheesecloth

1 tablespoon coarse salt

½ pound cooked ham

6 shallots

7 ounces white mushrooms

5 tablespoons olive oil

Salt and freshly ground black pepper

½ bunch chives

½ bunch parsley

½ tablespoon minced rosemary

½ tablespoon minced thyme

8 large tomatoes

Cut the carrots and onion into large chunks.

Place the hen, veal shank, and short ribs in a large stockpot. Cover with 3 quarts of water, bring to a boil, and cook for 5 minutes, skimming off any foam that rises to the surface. Add the carrots, onion, bouquet garni, and coarse salt. Cover, lower the heat, and simmer for 2½ hours. Remove the meats from the pot and set aside to cool.

When cool enough to handle, remove and discard the skin, fat, and bones from the hen, veal, and ribs. Finely mince the meat and place in a large mixing bowl. Cut the ham into ⅞-inch dice and stir into the mixing bowl. Refrigerate.

Mince the shallots and mushrooms.

Heat 3 tablespoons of the olive oil in a large skillet over low heat. Add the shallots and cook, stirring occasionally, for 10 minutes. Do not brown. Add the mushrooms, season with salt and pepper to taste, and cook for another 10 to 15 minutes, or until the moisture has evaporated and the mixture looks dry. Add the meats, stir well, and cook for a few minutes. Remove from the heat and allow to cool. Stir in the chives, parsley, rosemary, and thyme and adjust the seasoning.

Preheat the oven to 350°F.

Cut off the tops of the tomatoes and reserve them. Remove the seeds from the tomatoes with a small spoon. Stuff the tomatoes with the meat and place the tomatoes in a large baking dish. Cover with the reserved tomato tops and drizzle with the remaining 2 tablespoons olive oil. Bake for 30 minutes, then increase the oven temperature to 400°F and bake until the tomatoes are nicely golden. Serve immediately.

*Everyone enjoys this family-style entrée. Instead of using the usual sausage meat, try this flavorful stuffing of hen, veal, beef, and ham. You can serve the tomatoes with basmati rice flavored with the cooking juices.*

**Note:** You may use a 3-pound chicken instead of a hen; reduce the cooking time to 45 minutes if you do so.

# VEAL STEW

**For the stew:**

2 pounds boneless veal meat

1 medium leek

2 medium carrots

2 medium onions

1 celery rib

Bouquet garni (¼ bay leaf,
2 sprigs parsley, 1 sprig
thyme), tied in cheesecloth

1 tablespoon coarse salt

7 ounces small pearl onions

7 ounces white mushrooms

3 tablespoons unsalted
butter

1 teaspoon sugar

Salt and freshly ground
black pepper

**The sauce:**

4 tablespoons all-purpose
flour

3 tablespoons unsalted
butter

1 egg yolk

½ cup crème fraîche

Salt and freshly ground
black pepper

The day before making the stew, place the veal in a mixing bowl. Cover with cold water, then cover with plastic wrap and refrigerate overnight.

**Make the stew:** Drain the veal and place in a large pot. Cover with cold water, bring to a boil over high heat, and cook for 5 minutes, skimming off any foam that rises to the surface. Drain the veal in a colander and rinse under cold running water. Drain again.

Cut off the top green part of the leek, leaving some of it. Remove the root and any blemished outer leaves. Insert a sharp paring knife at the bottom of the leek about 2 inches above the root and cut through the entire length of the leek. Wash under running water, making sure to remove any dirt and sand in between the leaves. Dry with paper towels. Cut into large chunks.

Cut the carrots and onions into large chunks. Return the veal to the pot and add just enough water to cover. Add the leeks, carrots, onions, bouquet garni, and coarse salt. Bring to a boil over high heat, cover, lower the heat, and simmer for 1 hour.

Soak the pearl onions in warm water for a few minutes and peel them. Cut the mushrooms into 4 or 6 pieces, depending on their size. Place the pearl onions in a small saucepan. Cover with cold water and add 1½ tablespoons of butter and sugar. Season with salt and pepper and cook over medium heat for 20 minutes, or until soft. Transfer to a deep serving dish. Keep warm.

Heat the remaining 1½ tablespoons butter in a small skillet over high heat and sauté the mushrooms. Season with salt and pepper and drain in a colander. Add the mushrooms to the pearl onions and keep warm. Remove the veal from the pot with a slotted spoon and place on a serving dish. Keep warm. Strain the broth, return it to the pot, and bring to a boil.

**Make the sauce:** Combine the flour and butter in a large saucepan. Whisk vigorously until well combined. Add the hot

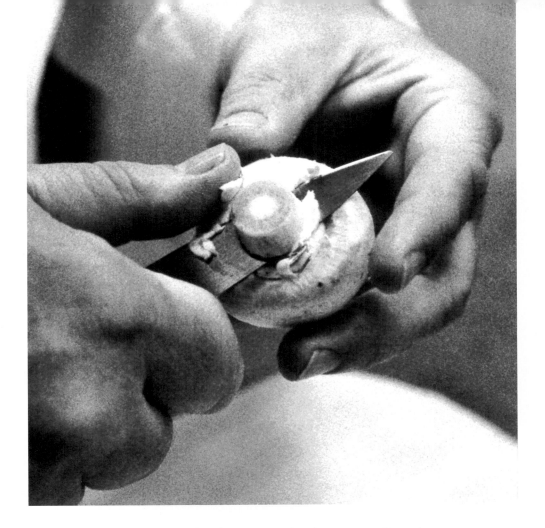

broth all at once and bring back to a boil over medium heat, whisking constantly. Simmer for at least 8 minutes, until slightly thickened. Remove from the heat.

Combine the egg yolk and crème fraîche in a small bowl. Slowly add the mixture to the broth, whisking constantly. Return to the heat and cook for a few minutes, until the broth starts to thicken. Season with salt and pepper to taste. Strain the sauce over the veal and serve immediately with steamed rice or vegetables such as carrots or zucchini.

*The roux, which is the base of this sauce, must remain colorless and should be cooked for as long as possible. The longer you cook it the better it will be.*

# GRILLED PORK RIBS
## WITH PEACHES

3 tablespoons unsalted butter

½ cup grapeseed or vegetable oil

4 pounds spareribs

8 slightly underripe yellow peaches

½ cup wine vinegar

½ cup cooking juices from a veal roast or veal stock (see recipe, page 137)

Salt and freshly ground black pepper

Fleur de sel

Preheat the oven to 400°F.

Heat 1½ tablespoons of the butter and the oil in a large skillet over high heat. Add the spareribs and cook they are well seared on all sides. Drain in a colander and place on a large baking sheet. Bake in the oven for 15 to 20 minutes.

Peel and quarter the peaches. Heat the remaining 1½ tablespoons butter over medium-high heat and cook the peaches for 2 minutes on each side. Add the vinegar and reduce by three-quarters. Add the veal juices or stock, reduce the heat to low, and cook for 3 to 4 minutes, until the peaches are well coated with the mixture. Season with salt and pepper to taste.

Divide the peaches among 4 individual serving plates. Cut the ribs into serving pieces and place on top of the peaches. Drizzle with the sauce, top with fleur de sel and freshly ground pepper, and serve.

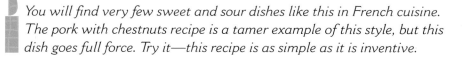

*You will find very few sweet and sour dishes like this in French cuisine. The pork with chestnuts recipe is a tamer example of this style, but this dish goes full force. Try it—this recipe is as simple as it is inventive.*

# CÔTE DE BOEUF
## WITH BÉARNAISE SAUCE
## AND THICK FRENCH FRIES

**For the béarnaise sauce:**

12 tablespoons unsalted butter

2 shallots

1 teaspoon white peppercorns, crushed

2 tablespoons minced tarragon

2 tablespoons minced chervil

3 egg yolks

Salt and freshly ground pepper

**For the beef and french fries:**

2 pounds Bintje potatoes (see Note)

Two 2-pound bone-in-rib-eye steaks

1 quart peanut oil

4 tablespoons unsalted butter

½ cup grapeseed or vegetable oil

Salt

Melt the butter in a small saucepan over medium heat. Remove from the heat and allow the milky residue to settle at the bottom of the pan. Carefully pour the clear yellow liquid into a bowl, leaving the residue behind. Set the clarified butter aside.

Peel the potatoes and cut them into thick sticks. Rinse them and place them in a bowl of cold water.

To make the béarnaise sauce, mince the shallots. Place them in a saucepan over low heat along the crushed pepper, vinegar and 1 tablespoon each of the tarragon and chervil. Simmer until the vinegar has evaporated. Add ¼ cup of cold water and set aside.

Heat the oil in a deep fryer to 325°F. Drain the potatoes and thoroughly dry them on paper towels. Place the potatoes in the basket of a deep fryer and fry in the hot oil for 3 to 4 minutes. Lift the basket from the oil and drain the french fries on paper towels.

To cook the steaks, melt the 4 tablespoons butter and the oil in a large, heavy skillet over medium-high heat. Sear the steaks for about 5 minutes on each side, or until golden brown, basting regularly with the cooking fat. Remove the meat to a rack and let it rest for 15 to 20 minutes.

To finish the béarnaise sauce, whisk the egg yolks into the reduced vinegar mixture. Place the saucepan over low heat and cook, whisking constantly, for 5 minutes. When the eggs become thick and you can see the bottom of the pan when you stir the sauce, whisk in the reserved clarified butter in a slow stream until the sauce is emulsified and thick. Season with salt and pepper to taste.

Return the french fries to the hot oil and cook until golden brown. Drain on paper towels. Transfer to a serving platter and season with salt.

Strain the sauce and stir in the remaining 1 tablespoon each of tarragon and chervil. Adjust the seasonings. Keep warm in a bain-marie or in a mixing bowl set over hot water.

Return the steaks to the skillet set over medium-high heat and cook for about 3 minutes on each side, or until heated through. Transfer the steaks to a cutting board.

Slice the steaks and serve with the french fries and béarnaise sauce on the side.

*If skinny french fries are great for nibbling, thick ones are meant for sinking your teeth into. The success of this recipe is in the timing. Everything should be ready at the same time—the final cooking of the meat, the french fries and, especially, the béarnaise sauce. This delicate sauce cannot bear waiting or being reheated.*

**Note:** The Bintje potato is a creamy, yellow-fleshed potato with a thin light brown skin. If they're not available, you may substitute all-purpose white or Yukon gold potatoes.

# BRAISED VEAL RUMP ROAST
## WITH CARROTS AND ONIONS

9 medium carrots

4 large onions

½ cup grapeseed or vegetable oil

4 tablespoons unsalted butter

One 2-pound veal rump roast

Salt and freshly ground black pepper

2 garlic cloves, peeled

Bouquet garni (¼ bay leaf, 2 sprigs parsley, 1 sprig thyme), tied in cheesecloth

Cut the carrots and onions into large pieces.

Preheat the oven to 400°F.

Heat the oil and butter in a heavy ovenproof pot over medium heat. Sear the veal until golden on both sides. Season with salt and pepper to taste and add the carrots, onions, garlic, and bouquet garni. Cover, place in the oven, and bake for 15 minutes. Add ½ cup water and bake another 20 minutes.

Transfer the meat to a cutting board. Remove the carrots and onions with a slotted spoon and keep warm. Strain the cooking juices.

Slice the veal and place it on a serving platter. Add the carrots and onions and spoon the cooking juices over them. Serve immediately.

*Rump roast is the best part of the veal. Try it, you'll see! Roasting brings out the full flavor of the veal. You can use the loin if you like, but there is no comparison.*

# LAMB STEW
## WITH SPRING VEGETABLES

5 ounces peas

5 ounces green beans

5 medium carrots

2 medium zucchini

4 turnips

1 medium onion

½ cup grapeseed oil

1 tablespoon unsalted butter

2 pounds lamb shoulder, boned

Salt and freshly ground black pepper

1 garlic clove

1 tablespoon tomato paste

Bouquet garni (¼ bay leaf, 2 sprigs parsley, 1 sprig thyme), tied in cheesecloth

Shell the peas and trim the beans. Cut one of the carrots, the zucchini, and turnips into 2-inch sticks. Set aside.

Cut the onion and remaining carrots into 1-inch pieces.

Heat the oil and butter in a large skillet over high heat. Sear the lamb until deep brown on all sides. Season with salt and pepper to taste. Place the meat in a large pot. Cover with 1 cup water, then add the carrot and onion pieces, the garlic, tomato paste, and bouquet garni. Bring to a boil, lower the heat to medium-low, and cook, covered, for 45 minutes.

Bring a large pot of salted water to a boil. Blanch the carrot sticks for 3 to 4 minutes, or until cooked through but still firm. Plunge in a bowl of ice water and drain. Repeat with the green beans, turnips, zucchini, and peas.

Remove the meat from the pot and set aside. Reduce the cooking liquid by one-quarter. Strain into a clean pot. Add the meat and vegetables to the reduced sauce; adjust the seasonings and cook for a few more minutes.

*This is a spring classic filled with the flavors of the young tender vegetables. Unlike other stews with their earthy tones, this one is very colorful, crisp, and pretty. So take extra care not to overcook the vegetables at the end so they keep their vibrancy.*

# CHICKEN STOCK

1 pound chicken necks
and wing tips

2 medium carrots

1 medium onion

1 celery rib

1 medium leek

Bouquet garni (¼ bay leaf,
2 sprigs parsley, 1 sprig
thyme), tied in cheesecloth

1 tablespoon coarse salt

Place the chicken necks and wing tips in a stockpot. Cover with water and bring to a boil. Boil for 5 minutes, skimming off any foam that rises to the surface. Lower heat and simmer for 15 minutes.

 Meanwhile, peel and rinse the vegetables. Halve the carrots, onion, celery, and leek lengthwise. Add them to the pot, along with the bouquet garni and salt. Cover and cook for 2 to 3 hours over low heat, skimming occasionally.

Strain through a chinois or a fine-mesh strainer and cool.

*This broth will keep 2 to 3 days in the refrigerator. It also may be frozen in ice cube trays and stored in the freezer in small plastic bags.*

# VEAL STOCK

Preheat the oven to 450°F.

Spread the veal bones on a baking sheet and roast until golden brown, 15 to 20 minutes.

Peel and rinse the vegetables and cut them in large chunks. Quarter the tomatoes.

Place the bones in a large stockpot along with the vegetables, tomatoes, and bouquet garni. Cover with 5 quarts of water. Bring to a boil and skim off any foam that rises to the surface. Lower the heat to a simmer and cook, covered, for 3 hours.

Strain through a chinois or a fine-mesh strainer and cool.

*This broth will keep 2 to 3 days in the refrigerator. It also may be frozen in ice cube trays and stored in the freezer in small plastic bags.*

2 to 4 pounds veal bones

2 medium carrots

3 medium onions

1 medium leek

3 medium tomatoes

Bouquet garni (¼ bay leaf, 2 sprigs parsley, 1 sprig thyme), tied in cheesecloth

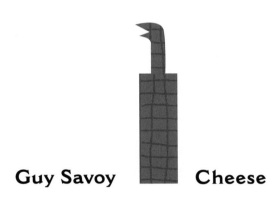

Guy Savoy      Cheese

# BEAUFORT CHEESE
## WITH FRESH HERB SALAD

½ bunch chives

½ bunch chervil

½ bunch Italian parsley

8 ounces Beaufort cheese

2 cups loosely packed green or red oak leaf lettuce

2 tablespoons Basic Vinaigrette (see recipe, page 50)

Salt and freshly ground black pepper

Cut the chives into ¾-inch pieces. Discard the stems of the chervil and parsley and reserve the leaves. Cut the cheese into very thin slices.

In a large bowl, toss the lettuce and the herbs with the vinaigrette. Season with salt and pepper to taste.

Place the salad in the center of 4 individual serving plates. Place the Beaufort slices over the salad.

*Beaufort is a full-flavored cheese with a complex, nutty aroma. This light, simple salad works well as a counterpart to the Beaufort. To add a fresh note and some crispness, you can toss a few thin apple slices into the salad.*

## ROASTED
## GOAT CHEESE

Preheat the oven to 400°F.

Cut the baguette on a bias into four ½-inch slices.

Peel the garlic clove and cut it in half. Rub both sides of the baguette slices with the garlic. Discard the garlic and place the slices on a baking sheet.

Heat the butter in a nonstick skillet over medium heat. When it starts to foam, add the goat cheese and cook for 10 seconds on each side.

Place the individual cheeses on top of the bread slices. Bake for 3 minutes, or until the cheese starts to melt. Serve immediately.

*A light salad of delicate greens such as lamb's lettuce makes a good accompaniment to this dish. It can be served either as a cheese course or an appetizer, and it's so good that it might even get your children eating cheese.*

½ baguette

1 garlic clove

1 tablespoon unsalted butter

4 crottins de Chavignol or other semi-dry individual goat cheeses, about 2 ounces each

# SAINT-MARCELLIN CHEESE
## WITH WALNUT CREAM

8 walnuts in the shell

3 tablespoons heavy cream

Salt and freshly ground black pepper

2 Saint-Marcellin cheeses (about 3½ ounces each), well aged and creamy

Walnut bread for serving

Shell the walnuts and coarsely chop them. Combine the walnuts with the cream in a small bowl. Season with salt and pepper. Halve the Saint-Marcellin cheeses and arrange them on 4 individual serving plates. Spoon some of the walnut-cream mixture along the side. Serve with slices of walnut bread.

*Saint-Marcellin should be served at room temperature. It's at its best when it is aged and mature and soft and runny inside. This cow's-milk cheese, produced in the Dauphiné region of France, was once made with goat's milk. It gained its reputation in the restaurant of La Mère Richard in Lyon, where the cheese was matured to a perfect creaminess.*

# CHEESE SOUFFÉ

4 tablespoons unsalted butter, plus more to butter the soufflé mold

4 tablespoons all-purpose flour, plus more for coating the mold

1 cup milk

3 egg yolks

4 egg whites

1 cup grated Gruyère cheese

Small pinch grated nutmeg

Salt and freshly ground pepper

Prepare a white roux by melting the butter in a medium saucepan over medium heat. Whisk in the flour, a little at a time, until well blended. Cook for 1 minute, whisking constantly. Pour into a small bowl, allow to cool, and refrigerate until the mixture is completely cold.

Preheat the oven to 350°F.

Bring the milk just to a boil in a small saucepan. Place the roux in a medium saucepan and pour the hot milk over it to make a béchamel. Slowly bring the mixture to a boil over medium heat, whisking constantly. Cook, continuing to whisk, for 3 to 4 minutes.

Remove the pan from the heat and whisk in the egg yolks, 1 at a time, mixing before each addition. Return the pan to the heat and cook for another minute, still whisking constantly. Set aside.

In an electric mixer, beat the egg whites until stiff peaks form. Place half of the béchamel mixture in a large mixing bowl. Fold half of the egg whites into the béchamel. Combine well. Then fold in the rest of the béchamel, the Gruyère, and the remaining egg whites, mixing well in between each addition. Season with the nutmeg and salt and pepper to taste.

Bring 1 quart of water to a boil in a medium saucepan. Lightly butter the bottom and sides of a 6-cup soufflé mold and dust with flour, shaking off any excess. Pour the batter into the mold. Place the mold in a roasting pan and pour in the boiling water to reach halfway up the sides. Bake for 35 minutes. Serve immediately.

*This cheese soufflé was always a wonder when I was growing up. It smelled good and looked good, and its moist, somewhat elastic consistency is one of my greatest childhood memories. Cheese soufflés are among the dishes that make children dream . . . and adults, too.*

**Guy Savoy**  **Desserts**

# RASPBERRY
## CLAFOUTIS

3 large eggs

¼ cup sugar, plus
1 teaspoon for coating
the dish

4 ounces crème fraîche

1 tablespoon raspberry
eau de vie (see Note)

½ pound fresh raspberries

Whisk the eggs, ¼ cup sugar, and crème fraîche together in a large mixing bowl until smooth and emulsified. Stir in the eau de vie.

Preheat the oven to 350°F.

Lightly butter a baking dish large enough to hold the raspberries in 1 layer. Sprinkle with the teaspoon of sugar and shake the pan to coat evenly. Layer the raspberries onto the dish. Pour the crème fraîche mixture over them. Bake for 20 minutes.

Remove from the oven and cool slightly. Serve warm with vanilla ice cream or fresh berry coulis.

*This dessert reminds me of the wild raspberries we harvested in the mountains near my childhood home. Small and fragrant, they made the most flavorful jellies and delicious desserts. We scratched our arms as we picked, but it was worth it.*

**Note:** Eau de vie is a clear, colorless brandy or spirit distilled from fermented fruit juices.

# SEASONAL FRUIT
## SKEWERS

1 pint strawberries

½ pineapple

1 mango

2 bananas

2 tablespoons acacia honey

Hull the strawberries, then rinse them and halve them lengthwise.

Peel the pineapple and mango. Cut the mango into 1-inch cubes. Cut the pineapple into 1-inch pieces over a bowl to collect the juices. Refrigerate until ready to use, reserving the pineapple juice.

Peel and cut the bananas into 1-inch slices.

Preheat the oven to 350°F degrees. Combine the honey and pineapple juice in a small bowl.

Arrange the fruits on 8-inch skewers, alternating them according to color and flavor. Place the skewers on a baking sheet and coat with the honey mixture. Bake for 5 to 10 minutes, or until the fruit is slightly caramelized.

Serve immediately with a fruit coulis or chocolate ice cream.

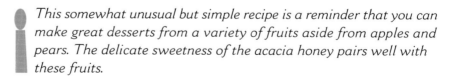

*This somewhat unusual but simple recipe is a reminder that you can make great desserts from a variety of fruits aside from apples and pears. The delicate sweetness of the acacia honey pairs well with these fruits.*

# POACHED PEARS
## IN RED WINE

Peel the pears and halve them. Remove the center core and seeds, and rub with lemon juice to keep the pears from discoloring.

Combine the wine, sugar, and vanilla bean in a large pot. Bring to a boil, stirring to dissolve the sugar, and add the pears. Lower the heat to medium and simmer for 15 minutes, or until the pears are tender. Cooking time may vary depending on the ripeness of the pears. Check for doneness by inserting a sharp paring knife into the thickest part of the flesh.

Using a slotted spoon, remove the pears and let cool for 30 minutes at room temperature. Transfer the pears and poaching liquid to a serving bowl. Place them in the refrigerator and chill for 3 hours.

To serve, arrange 2 pear halves in 4 individual soup bowls. Ladle some of the poaching liquid over them.

*This is a magnificent fall dessert. And why confine it to dessert—you can also serve it as a mid-afternoon snack. You can substitute another type of pear for the Bartlett as long as it is not too big. You may also use the poaching liquid to make a delicious granité (see Champagne Granité, page 176).*

4  Bartlett pears

Juice of 1 lemon

1 (75 cl) bottle red wine

1 cup sugar

1 vanilla bean, split in half

# RICE PUDDING

½ cup short-grain white rice

2½ cups milk

1¼ cups heavy cream

2 vanilla beans

¼ cup sugar

Place the rice in a large saucepan. Cover with cold water and bring to a boil. Remove from the heat and drain into a strainer.

Return the rice to the pan and add the milk and cream. Split the vanilla beans lengthwise and scrape the seeds with the tip of a paring knife. Add the pods and seeds to the saucepan. Bring to a boil over medium heat, reduce the heat to low, and simmer for 50 minutes, stirring occasionally with a wooden spoon to prevent the rice from sticking to the bottom of the pan.

Stir in the sugar and simmer for 10 more minutes. Pour the rice pudding into a small serving bowl, discarding the vanilla beans. Refrigerate for 2 hours. Serve the pudding at room temperature.

*For me, this is* the *dessert par* excellence. *It took me thirty years to come up with the nerve to put it on my dessert menu. Served as a petit four with a small spoon, you'll see it disappear very quickly.*

# WALNUT TART
## WITH VANILLA ICE CREAM

*For the pastry crust:*

1 cup all-purpose flour

Pinch salt

2 teaspoons sugar

1 egg yolk, beaten

½ cup unsalted butter, at
room temperature, cut into
small pieces, plus more for
buttering the mold

*For the filling:*

12 tablespoons unsalted
butter, at room temperature

½ cup sugar

3 eggs

¾ cup sifted all-purpose
flour

3 ounces walnut, coarsely
chopped

*For the ice cream:*

4 egg yolks

6 tablespoons sugar

2½ cups milk

2 vanilla beans

**Prepare the dough:** Sift the flour and salt into a large mixing bowl and create a well in the center. Add the sugar and yolk to the well and stir them into the flour with a fork. Quickly rub the butter into the flour with your fingers until the mixture is crumbly and just holds together. Gather the dough into a ball and place it on a lightly floured work surface. Knead for 2 to 3 minutes, or until smooth. Wrap the dough in plastic and refrigerate for 1 hour.

Lightly butter a 9-inch tart mold with a removable bottom. Place the dough on a lightly floured board and roll it out into a circle about 11 inches in diameter and ⅛ inch thick. Carefully line the prepared mold with the dough. Trim off the excess dough.

Preheat the oven to 350°F.

**Prepare the filling:** Place the butter and sugar in the bowl of an electric mixer. Beat until the mixture is light and fluffy. Add the eggs, 1 at the time, beating until well incorporated before each addition. Fold in the flour and walnuts using a rubber spatula.

Remove the tart shell from the refrigerator and pour in the filling. Bake for 20 minutes. Allow the tart to cool for 1 hour before removing it from the mold.

**Prepare the vanilla ice cream:** Place the egg yolks and sugar in the bowl of an electric mixer. Beat until the mixture is light, fluffy, and pale yellow in color. Place the milk in a small saucepan. Split the vanilla beans lengthwise and scrape the seeds with the tip of a paring knife. Add the pods and seeds to the saucepan. Bring just to a boil, then remove from the heat, discard the vanilla beans, and slowly pour into the egg and sugar mixture, whisking constantly. Set aside to cool. Pour into the bowl of an ice cream machine and churn according to the manufacturer's directions.

Serve the tart warm with a scoop of vanilla ice cream on top.

Nothing is more "Dauphinois" than the walnut tart. This pastry,
a childhood favorite, showcases the delicious walnuts of this region.
Stick with walnuts in the shell, as store-bought shelled walnuts are
often rancid.

# BRIOCHE FRENCH TOAST
## WITH PINK PRALINES

1½ cups milk

2 tablespoons sugar

2 egg yolks

1 whole egg

3 tablespoons pink pralines
(see Note)

1 brioche loaf

8 tablespoons unsalted
butter

In a small saucepan heat the milk until just warm. Beat the sugar, egg yolks and egg together in a large mixing bowl. Slowly add the milk, whisking constantly, until well combined. Strain the mixture into a shallow dish and set aside.

Coarsely chop the pralines.

Remove and discard the ends of the brioche loaf and cut into ¾-inch slices. Dip each slice in the batter and place on a large platter.

Heat the butter in a nonstick skillet over medium heat. Add a few brioche slices, making sure not to crowd the pan, and cook until golden on both sides. Repeat with the remaining brioche slices.

Place the brioche slices on a serving platter and sprinkle with the chopped pink pralines. Serve immediately.

*The brioche from Bourgoin-Jallieu near Lyons is decorated with two types of sugar, one red and the other white. Pink pralines are nestled in the white side, white almond candy on the red side. The childhood memories of this specialty (and others in the region such as pralines from Saint-Genix) inspired me to create this dessert. You may serve it with crème Anglaise or vanilla ice cream.*

**Note:** Pralines are sugar-coated almonds or hazelnuts, and they are available at specialty stores. If you can't find pink pralines, you may substitute caramel-colored ones.

# APPLE TART

**For the pastry crust:**

1½ cup all-purpose flour

Pinch salt

2 teaspoons sugar

1 egg yolk, beaten

½ cup unsalted butter, at room temperature, cut into small pieces, plus more for buttering the mold

**For the filling:**

1¼ pounds firm-crisp apples, such as Boskoop or Cortland

1½ tablespoons sugar

**Prepare the dough:** Sift the flour and salt into a large mixing bowl and create a well in the center. Add the sugar and egg yolk to the well and stir them into the flour with a fork. Quickly rub the butter into the flour with your fingers, until the mixture is crumbly and just holds together. Gather the dough into a ball and place it on a lightly floured work surface. Knead for 2 to 3 minutes, or until smooth. Wrap the dough in plastic wrap and refrigerate for 1 hour.

**Prepare the filling:** Peel and halve half of the apples. Remove the center cores and cut into very thin slices. Place the slices in a medium saucepan over medium-low heat, stir in the sugar, and cook, stirring occasionally, until the apples break down into a compote, about 20 minutes. Strain through a fine-mesh strainer and set aside.

Lightly butter a 9-inch tart mold with a removable bottom. Place the dough on a lightly floured surface and roll it out into a circle about 11 inches in diameter and ⅛ inch thick. Carefully line the prepared mold with the dough. Trim off the excess dough from around the rim of the pan.

Preheat the oven to 400°F.

Peel the remaining apples, halve them, and remove the center cores. Cut into very thin slices.

Spread the apple compote over the bottom of the tart shell in an even layer. Arrange the apple slices on top in a concentric circle. Bake for 20 minutes. Remove the ring from the mold and bake for 10 to 15 additional minutes.

Allow the tart to cool for 1 hour before removing it from the mold and serving.

*The scent of butter and sugar caramelizing in the oven—apple tarts are all about smell. In my home, these luscious aromas came after the just as enticing ones of the Sunday roasted chicken (see recipe, page 108). To achieve the perfect harmony between the sweet crispness of the dough and the acidity of the apple, use a crisp, sweet, tart apple.*

# CRÊPES WITH
## CITRUS FRUIT

1 cup all-purpose flour

2 tablespoons plus ½ teaspoon sugar

Pinch salt

2 whole eggs

1½ cups milk

3 tablespoons unsalted butter, melted

2 organic oranges

1 organic grapefruit

Sift the flour into a large mixing bowl and create a well in the center. Place 2 tablespoons of the sugar, salt, and the eggs into the well. Slowly start whisking the ingredients together, adding the milk, a little at a time, blending well after each addition to avoid forming any lumps. Keep whisking and adding the milk until the batter is smooth and homogenous.

Stir 2 tablespoons of the melted butter into the batter. Strain into a clean bowl and set aside at room temperature for 1 hour.

Bring a medium pot of water to a boil. Rinse and dry the oranges and grapefruit. Using a vegetable peeler, remove the rind of 1 orange and one-quarter of the grapefruit. Be careful not to remove the bitter white pith. Blanch the rind in boiling water for 1 minute. Drain and cool under running water. Repeat twice. Dry the rind on paper towels and finely mince. Add the minced rind to the crêpe batter.

Peel the oranges and grapefruit, cutting through the pith and exposing the flesh. Working over a bowl to collect the juices, cut out the sections in between the membranes. Reserve the pieces in a separate bowl. Squeeze what is left of the oranges and grapefruits to extract the juices.

In a medium saucepan over medium heat, cook the orange and grapefruit juices with ½ teaspoon of the sugar and reduce by half. Set aside to cool.

Heat a 6-inch nonstick crêpe pan or skillet over medium heat. Brush with some of the remaining melted butter. Ladle about ¼ cup of the batter into the pan, tilting the pan in a circular motion to distribute the batter evenly. Cook until the batter is set, then flip the crêpe and cook a minute longer. Remove to a plate and cover with aluminum foil to keep warm. Repeat until all the batter has been used, brushing on more butter as necessary.

To serve, arrange the orange and grapefruit wedges on individual serving plates. Fold the crêpes into fourths and place them alongside the fruit. Drizzle with the reserved syrup.

*Everyone loves crêpes Suzette. In this version, the acidity of the orange is combined with the bitterness of the grapefruit. The success of the recipe comes from the delicate lightness of the crêpes, so make sure the batter bubbles as soon as it hits the pan—too often crêpes can be mistaken for plaster.*

# BAKED APPLES
## WITH DRIED FRUITS

4 Boskoop apples or any firm-crisp variety such as Cortland

Butter to grease the dish

1 tablespoon walnuts

1 tablespoon hazelnuts

5 dried apricots

3 prunes, pitted

1 tablespoon golden raisins

1 tablespoon brown sugar

Cut off the tops of the apples and reserve them. Remove the core and some of the flesh. Set aside.

Preheat the oven to 400°F. Butter a baking dish large enough to hold the apples.

Mince the walnuts, hazelnuts, apricots, prunes, and raisins and combine them in a small mixing bowl. Stuff the apples with the mixture, then place the apples in the prepared baking dish.

Bake for 15 to 20 minutes, then sprinkle the sugar over the fruit and nut mixture. Cover with the reserved apple tops and bake for another 20 to 25 minutes. Serve hot.

*In my family, this dessert was a good way to add sophistication to the sometimes boring baked apples, where hazelnuts and walnuts were always abundant. You can refine this dessert by serving it with a scoop of vanilla, cinnamon, or caramel ice cream or a spoonful of crème fraîche.*

# CRÈME BRÛLÈE

2½ cups heavy cream

2 vanilla beans

⅓ cup sugar

6 egg yolks

2 tablespoons brown sugar

Place the heavy cream in a small saucepan over medium heat. Split the vanilla beans lengthwise and scrape off the seeds with a paring knife. Add the seeds and pods to the cream. Slowly bring the mixture to a boil, cover the pan, and remove from the heat. Let the vanilla infuse the cream for 20 minutes.

Preheat the oven to 300°F.

In the bowl of an electric mixer, whisk the sugar and egg yolks together until the mixture is thick and pale yellow. Remove the vanilla pods from the cream. Slowly add the cream in a steady stream to the egg mixture, whisking constantly.

Strain the mixture and pour into 4 shallow 4½-inch-wide ramekins. Set the ramekins in a baking dish and pour hot water into it to within 1 inch of the top of the ramekins. Bake for 1¾ hours to 2 hours, or until the cream just sets but slightly wobbles. Remove from the oven and allow to cool, then wrap with plastic and chill. Just before serving, sprinkle the top of the cream with the brown sugar and place under the broiler until caramelized, turning the ramekins as necessary

*To caramelize the custard, my parents used to use a big iron disk with a long handle heated over an open flame. Slow even cooking is key to this recipe—don't try to rush it.*

# BITTER CHOCOLATE
## SORBET

Cut the bittersweet chocolate into small pieces.

Combine the sugar and water in a small saucepan, and bring to a boil over medium heat. Add the cocoa powder and stir until dissolved. Add the chocolate pieces and stir until the mixture is thick and smooth. Remove from the heat and set aside to cool.

Pour into an ice cream machine and churn according to the manufacturer's directions.

Using 2 large spoons, shape the sorbet into small quenelles and serve with madeleines or sugar cookies.

*I didn't always like bittersweet chocolate—like most children, I preferred the sweetness of the lighter milk chocolate, but I started to appreciate the more robust types of chocolate during my teenage years. This sorbet recipe is so simple that it would a shame to deny yourself this treat.*

3½ ounces bittersweet chocolate (70% cocoa)

¼ cup sugar

1 cup water

1½ ounces cocoa powder

Madeleines (see recipe, page 184), optional

Sugar cookies (see recipe, page 182), optional

# QUINCE PASTE

1 lemon

1¼ pounds quince

About 13 ounces sugar

½ cup water

2 tablespoons fine
crystallized sugar

Rinse and scrub the lemon. Remove the zest using a vegetable peeler and reserve.

Peel the quince and discard the core and seeds. Weigh the remaining fruit. You should have an equal weight of sugar to the peeled and seeded quince, so use more or less sugar as needed.

Place the quince, lemon zest, and water in a large pot over high heat. Bring to a boil, stirring occasionally with a wooden spoon. Lower the heat and simmer for 25 minutes, or until the quince falls apart and turns into a soft puree.

Add the measured sugar and cook for 5 minutes, stirring constantly. Pour the mixture into a large shallow dish in a layer about 1 inch thick. Allow to cool and then refrigerate for 4 hours to set.

Cut the quince paste into 2-inch cubes and roll it in the crystallized sugar. Serve as a snack or sweet just after a meal.

*This is the queen of fruit pastes and the quintessence of the quince. It has everything—the flavor, the unctuous consistency, the balance between sweet and sour, the fruity acidity. For added body, tie a cheesecloth around the quince peels and cores and add them to the pot. Remove them just before pouring the mixture into the dish.*

# CHOCOLATE MOUSSE

7 ounces bittersweet
chocolate (70% cocoa)

1 cup heavy cream, chilled

Sugar cookies (see recipe,
page 182), optional

Cut the chocolate into small pieces and place them in the top part of a bain-marie or in a mixing bowl set over a pot of hot water. Bring the water to a simmer over low heat and melt the chocolate, stirring occasionally with a rubber spatula.

Meanwhile, bring ½ cup of the cream to a boil, keeping the rest in the refrigerator. Whisk the hot cream into the melted chocolate until smooth and creamy. Set aside to cool for a few minutes.

In the bowl of an electric mixer, whip the ½ cup cream until light, fluffy, and firm. Using a rubber spatula, carefully fold the whipped cream, a little at a time, into the chocolate mixture. Blend well in between each addition. Pour the mixture into a serving bowl or individual ramekins and refrigerate for 2 hours.

Remove the mousse from the refrigerator about 10 minutes before serving. Serve with sugar cookies.

*Just like my bitter chocolate sorbet recipe, this chocolate mousse is very simple to make. Unlike most mousse recipes made with eggs and butter, this is a very quick recipe, almost like an airy ganache with a pleasingly intense chocolate flavor.*

# CHAMPAGNE GRANITÉ
## WITH RED BERRIES

3 tablespoons sugar

3 tablespoons water

½ bottle brut Champagne

1 pint strawberries

1 pint raspberries

1 pint fresh red currants

2 teaspoons confectioners' sugar

Combine the sugar and water in a small saucepan and bring to a boil over high heat. Remove from the heat and set aside to cool.

Add the Champagne to the sugar and water mixture and pour into a shallow pan in a 1-inch-deep layer. Place in the freezer for 2 hours, stirring the mixture with a fork every 20 minutes.

Hull the strawberries and halve or quarter them depending on their size.

Layer the strawberries at the center of 4 chilled individual serving plates. Cover with some of the granité. Scatter the raspberries and currants around the granité and dust with the confectioners' sugar. Serve immediately.

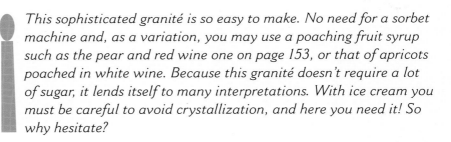

*This sophisticated granité is so easy to make. No need for a sorbet machine and, as a variation, you may use a poaching fruit syrup such as the pear and red wine one on page 153, or that of apricots poached in white wine. Because this granité doesn't require a lot of sugar, it lends itself to many interpretations. With ice cream you must be careful to avoid crystallization, and here you need it! So why hesitate?*

# FLOATING ISLAND

4 egg whites

Pinch salt

1 cup sugar

2½ cups milk

1 vanilla bean

3 egg yolks

Place the egg whites and salt in the bowl of an electric mixer. Whip the egg whites until they form soft peaks. Add ½ cup of the sugar and whip again until the egg whites are firm and shiny.

Pour the milk into a medium saucepan over medium heat. Split the vanilla bean in half and scrape the seeds with a paring knife. Add the pod and seeds to the milk, and slowly bring the milk to a boil. Reduce the heat until the temperature reaches 150°F on a candy thermometer.

Shape the meringue into quenelles using 2 large spoons. Carefully poach them in the milk for 1 minute on each side. To ensure even cooking, poach 3 pieces of the meringue at the same time. Drain on paper towels and repeat until all the meringue is used. Set aside in a cool place.

Strain the milk and reserve for the crème Anglaise.

**Make the crème Anglaise:** Beat the egg yolks with the remaining ½ cup sugar in a large mixing bowl until the mixture is thick and pale yellow. Bring the milk back to a boil and pour it over the egg yolks, whisking constantly. Return the mixture to the saucepan and cook over medium-low heat, stirring constantly, until the mixture thickens and coats the back of the spoon. Strain into a bowl and refrigerate for 2 hours.

Spoon some the crème Anglaise into 4 individual serving bowls. Top with 2 poached egg whites and spoon additional crème over them.

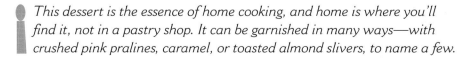

*This dessert is the essence of home cooking, and home is where you'll find it, not in a pastry shop. It can be garnished in many ways—with crushed pink pralines, caramel, or toasted almond slivers, to name a few.*

Preparation Time: **20 minutes**
+ 3 hours in the freezer

Cooking Time: **25 minutes**

# APRICOT COMPOTE
## WITH ORGEAT SYRUP SORBET

Halve the apricots and discard the pits.

Place the apricots in a large saucepan along with 2 tablespoons of the sugar, the water, and lemon juice over high heat. Bring to a boil, stirring constantly with a wooden spoon. Lower the heat and simmer for 15 to 20 minutes, stirring occasionally, until apricots break down into a chunky puree. Set aside to cool.

Place the milk and the remaining 7 tablespoons sugar in a medium saucepan and bring just to a boil. Remove from the heat and set aside to cool. Stir in the orgeat syrup and pour into a large shallow pan in a 1-inch-deep layer. Place in the freezer for 3 hours, stirring the mixture with a fork every 20 minutes.

Spoon some of the apricot compote into 4 individual serving dishes and top with a scoop of the orgeat sorbet.

1 pound very ripe apricots

9 tablespoons sugar

1 cup water

Juice of 1 lemon

1 quart milk

1 cup orgeat syrup
(see Note)

*Apricots are my favorite summer fruit, beautiful to look at and pleasing to the touch. The Dauphiné and Drôme regions of France are apricot kingdom, and these trees grew only few kilometers from my house. The apricot is always good regardless of its preparation— just plain, in a compote or a tart, as a sorbet, jam, or paste— anything you like. The orgeat syrup here highlights the fruit's affinity with almonds.*

**Note:** Orgeat syrup is made from almonds with a flavoring such as rose water or orange blossom water.

# SUGAR COOKIES

8 tablespoons unsalted butter, at room temperature

7 tablespoons sugar

2 eggs

1 cup all-purpose flour, sifted

1 vanilla bean

Place the butter in a large mixing bowl and beat to a creamy consistency with a wooden spoon. Add the sugar, beating constantly until well blended. Beat in the eggs, 1 at a time, and then fold in the flour. Blend until the mixture is smooth and homogenous.

Split the vanilla bean lengthwise and scrape the seeds into the batter with a paring knife and stir well to blend.

Preheat the oven to 400°F.

Spoon the batter into the pocket of a pastry bag fitted with a plain tip. Pipe the batter onto a nonstick cookie sheet in straight lines about 2 inches long. Leave about $1\frac{1}{4}$ inches in between each row, as the batter will expand as it bakes. Bake for about 5 minutes, or until the edges of the cookies are golden brown. Carefully remove the cookies with a spatula and place on a rack to cool.

When the cookies have cooled, they may be stored in an airtight container until ready to use. Serve with ice cream or sorbet, or as a petit four with coffee at the end of a meal.

*It was with these cookies that the revelation of the magic of baking came to me as a very young child. Baking starts with ingredients that on their own bring no pleasure. Have you ever tried to taste a tablespoon of flour? It's the association of the ingredients that creates the magic. Just watch as the little strips of batter spread out on the cookie sheet, slowly browning around the edges, and then becoming crisp a few moments after they leave the oven . . . not to mention the smell!*

Preparation Time: **20 minutes**
Cooking Time: **15 minutes**

# MADELEINES

1 cup sugar

6 eggs

¼ cup milk

1½ cups sifted all-purpose flour, plus more for the molds

1 teaspoon baking powder

8 tablespoons unsalted butter, melted and cooled, plus more to butter the molds

Combine the sugar, eggs, and milk in a medium saucepan over medium heat and whisk until the eggs are frothy and start to thicken. Remove from the heat, pour into a mixing bowl, and continue whisking until the mixture cools.

Preheat the oven to 400°F. Slide the oven rack to the lowest level so the madeleine molds will be close to the heat.

Using a rubber spatula, fold in the flour and baking powder. Beat in the butter a little at a time until well incorporated. Set aside for 10 minutes.

Lightly brush the molds with melted butter and dust with flour. Shake off any excess.

Spoon the batter into the molds, filling them no more than three-quarters full. Bake for 10 minutes, or until firm.

Unmold the madeleines as soon as they come out of the oven and place on a rack to cool. Serve with a fresh fruit salad or chocolate mousse.

*Madeleines are the moist version of the sugar cookies on page 182, and similarly bring out the magic in baking. It is always a pleasure to discover them, plump and golden, as they come out of the oven.*

# INDEX

# ACKNOWLEDGMENTS

A big thank you to Sylvie Désormière for the strength of her opinions, her tenacity, her creativity, and her endless joie de vivre that made producing this book a constant pleasure.

Armed with so many talents, I obviously could not refuse her anything:

• Not the daily drafting of most of my kitchen staff, whom I warmly thank: Michel Roncière, Laurent Soliveres, Gilles Chesneau, Hugues Pouget, and foremost, Emmanuel Monsallier, who prepared most of the dishes.

• Nor the frequent seizing of my very efficient assistants, whom I sincerely thank: Francine Boissin and Nadine Delsarte.

• Nor the regular invasion of my office as a favorite site for photo shoots.

With Sylvie Désormière's formidable team, I enjoyed some unparalleled collaborations with artistic director Elisabeth Ferté, recipe editor Barbara Sabatier, and Sophie Brissaud, a brilliant editor and long-time accomplice.

I also want to thank Laurence Mouton and her stylist Corrine Morin, whose photographic talent I was very impressed with. I would also like to take this opportunity to congratulate them on having tasted all the dishes they so brilliantly photographed.

A big sincere thank you to all of you.

**Guy Savoy**

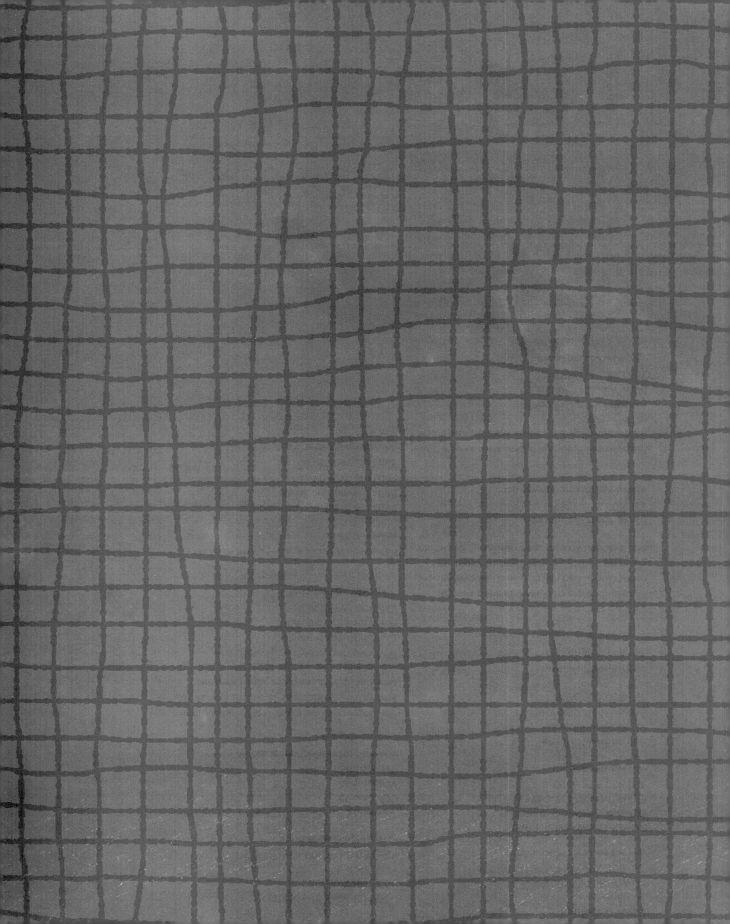

# SHOPPING

For a wide variety of olive oils, nuts oils, vinegars, salts, peppers, olives, sugars, vanilla beans, and much more, contact the following companies for information:

**Dean & Deluca**
560 Broadway
New York, NY 10012
Tel: 800.221.7714
www.deananddeluca.com

**Sweet Celebrations Inc.**
P.O. Box 39426
Edina, MN 55439-0426
Tel: 800.328.6722
www.sweetc.com

**Salumeria Italiana**
151 Richmond Street
Boston, MA 02109-1414
Tel: 800.400.5916

**Williams-Sonoma**
Tel: 877.812.6235
www.williams-sonoma.com

For a selection of classic French stocks, reductions, and sauces, such as demiglace, glace de viande, concentrated vegetable and seafood stocks, and rendered duck fat:

**More than Gourmet**
Tel: 800.860.9389
www.morethangourmet.com

For seasonal French produce, such as wild mushrooms, lamb's lettuce, truffles, and more:

**Marché Aux Délices**
New York, NY 10028
Tel: 888.547.5471
www.auxdelices.com

For a broad range of domestic and imported cheeses, fromage blanc (which freezes well so you could buy in quantity), crème fraîche, rich, cultured butter, and other dairy products:

**Ideal Cheese Shop, LTD.**
942 First Avenue
New York, NY 10022
Tel: 800.382.0109
www.idealcheese.com

**Vermont Butter and Cheese Company**
P.O. Box 95
Websterville, VT 05678
Tel: 800.884.6287
www.vbutterandcheeseco.com

For domestic foie gras; fresh ducks, geese, and game; French garlic sausages, tasty terrines, pâtés, and prepared entrees:

**D'Artagnan**
152 East 46th Street
New York, NY 10017
Tel: 800.DARTAGN
www.dartagnan.com

For succulent sea scallops and excellent seasonal fish:

**Browne Trading Company**
260 Commerical Street
Portland, ME 04101
Tel: 800.944.7878
www.browne-trading.com

Text and Photographs copyright © 2003 Editions Minerva,
Genève (Suisse)
Edited by Sophie Brissaud
Designed by Elisabeth Ferté

Published in 2004 by
Stewart, Tabori & Chang
A Company of La Martinière Groupe
115 West 18th Street
New York, NY 10011

Originally Published by
Editions Minerva
A Company of La Martinière Groupe
2 Rue de Christine
Paris, France 70056

Export Sales to all countries except Canada, France,
and French-speaking Switzerland:
Thames and Hudson Ltd.
181A High Holborn
London WC1V 7QX
England

Canadian Distribution:
Canadian Manda Group
One Atlantic Avenue, Suite 105
Toronto, Ontario M6K 3E7
Canada

Library of Congress Cataloging-in-Publication Data
is on file with the Library of Congress.

ISBN: 1-58479-362-7

Printed in Italy

10 9 8 7 6 5 4 3 2 1

First Printing